LIVING OUT YOUR
FAITH

Messages from the Gospel of John, Vol. III

LIVING OUT YOUR

FAITH

Messages from the Gospel of John, Vol. III

GREG LAURIE

ALLEN
DAVID
BOOKS

KERYGMA™
PUBLISHING   Dana Point, California

Living Out Your Faith

Unless otherwise indicated, all Scripture quotations are taken from the New King James Version. Copyright © 1982 by Thomas Nelson, Inc. Used by permission. All rights reserved.

Scripture quotations marked (NLT) are taken from the *Holy Bible*, New Living Translation, copyright © 1986. Used by permission of Tyndale House Publishers, Inc., Wheaton, Illinois 60189. All rights reserved.

Scripture quotations marked (NIV) are taken from THE HOLY BIBLE, NEW INTERNATIONAL VERSION (North American Edition). Copyright © 1973, 1978, 1984 by International Bible Society. Used by permission of Zondervan Publishing House.

ISBN 0-9777103-2-7

Printed in the United States of America.

Published by: Kerygma Publishing, Dana Point, California
Coordination: FM Management, Ltd.
Cover design: Christopher Laurie
Editing: Karla Pedrow
Interior Design: Highgate Cross+Cathey, Ltd.

"But go find my brothers and tell them that I am ascending to my Father and your Father, my God and your God."

John 20:17 NLT

Contents

1

THE LAST
SUPPER

John 13

I have a confession to make. I am beginning to despise cell phones. When cell phone technology first came into being, I was so excited. At first, you could get them for your car, which seemed amazing. Think of talking to someone from your car! Next they figured out how to fit a mobile phone into a briefcase (you had to have room for the battery and all that went with it). Then the first portable cell phone came out. I remember, because I was having lunch with a friend of mine who said, "Look what I have!" He proceeded to pull out the latest tech in cellular communication—a wireless phone about the size of a World War II walkie-talkie. It had a battery life of approximately an hour. Even so, I was dazzled by the technology. Of course, they have become a lot smaller since then. Now they are the size of a stick of gum, or so it seems.

But let me tell you why I despise cell phones: Almost everyone has them, and they use them almost everywhere. The reason these little technological wonders can be so annoying is because people don't seem to have cell phone etiquette. Have you ever been in the middle of a conversation with someone when his or her cell phone rang? *Hello? Yeah. Uh, no, I'm not with anyone important. Go ahead. No, I have all day. Yeah, go ahead*.... Meanwhile, you are sitting there, picking lint off your sleeve. It's a little awkward, isn't it? Then there are those who carry on extended cell-phone conversations in their cars, driving like they are intoxicated. You can always tell who they are, because while everyone else is clipping along, they are typically going about ten miles per hour and often cutting someone else off in the process. And what do you think these people on their cell phones are saying to the people they are speaking to? "Hey! I almost hit some guy!"

Cell phones have affected the animal kingdom as well. I read an article about a city in Denmark where many birds are changing the way they sing.

They've begun imitating the sound of cell phones ringing. One man even gave the name Nokia to a cell-phone mimicking bird in his garden. It's imitation at its worst.

THE ULTIMATE IMITATOR

Even so, we are about to look at a person who was an imitator extraordinaire, one of the most mysterious and paradoxical individuals ever found in the pages of Scripture: Judas Iscariot. His very name is synonymous with evil and treachery. He was the traitor's traitor. His life ended miserably in suicide, because he sold out Jesus for thirty pieces of silver. But there is more to Judas than that.

You might be surprised to know that Judas would appear rather upright.

If we were to have met Judas back then, he wouldn't have come across as the sinister, evil man we would expect (outwardly, at least). In most movies about the life of Christ, we always know who Judas is, because he is the sinister-looking one. All the disciples are in light-colored robes, while Judas is in a black robe (maybe black leather with the collar turned up), always lurking in the shadows.

Jesus was the ultimate example, to say the least.

So we think, *If I went back to the time of Christ and saw the disciples, I could pick Judas out right away.* But I don't know about that. I think we might be surprised. I would suggest that if we were to see the disciples for the first time, we would have a hard time knowing who Judas was, because he would have stood out. But it wouldn't have been in the way we might think.

You might be surprised to know that Judas would appear rather upright, seemingly considerate, and very religious. Remember his loud protest over Mary's so-called waste as she anointed the feet of Jesus with the costly oil (see John 12:1–6)? That appeared so considerate and compassionate on his part, but in reality, as John points out, he said this not because he cared about the poor, but because he was keeping the money and pocketing some of it as well.

Judas was an actor, and in fact, the first of many who are tremendous actors in the church today. They talk the talk, carry Bibles, and sing the songs. But underneath, they are phony. And they are fooling only themselves. Here in John 13, we will learn about that and more.

LOVING TO THE END

At this point in Jesus' ministry, His hour has now come. It is the hour of His arrest, His suffering, His crucifixion, and His resurrection. In fifteen to eighteen hours from the events recorded for us in John 13, our Lord would be suspended between heaven and Earth as He bore the sins of humanity. We come to the last Passover service Jesus would celebrate with His disciples, along with the first-ever Communion service. We catch a closing glimpse of Judas before he slinks into the night with betrayal on his mind. We take a somewhat comical look at Simon Peter as Jesus tries to wash his feet. Finally, we get a better look at ourselves as we discover more about what Jesus desires for us.

It all begins with a powerful opening verse:

Now before the Feast of the Passover, when Jesus knew that His hour had come that He

should depart from this world to the Father,
having loved His own who were in the
world, He loved them to the end. (v. 1)

The disciples were alone with Jesus. The crowds
were gone, along with all the pushing and pulling
that accompanied Jesus. The world was locked
out, and the disciples relaxed around a low-slung
table. But something was up. They could clearly see
that Jesus was troubled. Very troubled. Something
wasn't right, but no one knew quite what. Then
Jesus did something completely unexpected:

And supper being ended, the devil having
already put it into the heart of Judas Iscariot,
Simon's son, to betray Him, Jesus, knowing
that the Father had given all things into His
hands, and that He had come from God and
was going to God, rose from supper and laid
aside His garments, took a towel and girded
Himself. After that, He poured water into a
basin and began to wash the disciples' feet,
and to wipe them with the towel with which
He was girded. (vv. 2–5)

With all the pressure of Calvary closing in, this
is a touching and disarming portrait of Christ as He
washed the disciples' feet, loving them to the end.
Assuming the role of a household servant, Jesus
removed His outer garment and began to wash

their feet. We've heard of "throwing in the towel," but in this case, Jesus was picking it up. Perhaps as He dried the feet of Andrew and Mark, He thought, *These precious feet will spread the gospel to the world!* Perhaps the words of the prophet Isaiah came to mind: "How beautiful upon the mountains are the feet of him who brings good news..." (Isa. 52:7).

Then He came to the feet of Judas Iscariot, knowing that the very feet He was washing would soon steal away in the dark to betray Him.

Then Jesus came to the feet of the outspoken fisherman, Simon Peter.

Peter protested, "Lord, are You washing my feet?" (v. 6).

He washed the disciples' feet, loving them to the end.

It seemed that sometimes Peter opened his mouth only to switch feet. But I don't think Peter was being disrespectful. He just didn't understand. You see, this was the role of a servant. If you were a relatively affluent person living in that time, you would have a household servant whose job it was, among other things, to wash the feet of someone who came to your home. Jesus was behaving like a servant. So Peter was protesting. *You are the Master, not just of the house, but of the universe. Why are You washing my feet?*

But Jesus told him, "If I do not wash you, you have no part with Me" (v. 8).

Once Peter grasped this, he wanted Jesus to give him a bath: "Lord, not my feet only, but also my hands and my head!" (v. 9).

They were willing to fight for the throne, but no one wanted the towel.

It's kind of humorous, really. But Jesus was being an example. He was demonstrating to them that if they wanted to be greatest in the kingdom of God, they must be the servant of all (see Mark 9:35). And later, He would instruct them to do this for one another—to serve one another, help one another, and prefer one another. Ironically, Luke's Gospel tells us that an argument broke out in Jesus' presence as to who would be the greatest in the Kingdom (see Luke 9:24–27). Talk about missing the point. They were willing to fight for the throne, but no one wanted the towel.

THE TRAITOR IN THEIR MIDST

But Jesus was troubled by something far worse than their silly bickering:

When Jesus had said these things, He was troubled in spirit, and testified and said, "Most assuredly, I say to you, one of you will betray Me." Then the disciples looked at one another, perplexed about whom He spoke. (vv. 21–22)

Talk about dropping a bombshell! The fact that Jesus was troubled would, in itself, be troubling to the disciples. After all, Jesus was always the calm in the midst of the storm, sometimes even literally as He controlled the weather simply with His voice. He was always the one with the right words, the right deeds … the right everything. Yet here He was, "troubled" (v. 21). This is the same word used previously in John 11:33 when Jesus stood by the grave of Lazarus and wept. It is also the same word Jesus used in John 12:27 to describe His thoughts about His impending death on the cross.

Jesus was fully God, but He also was fully man. Therefore, certain things troubled Him. He knew anger and sorrow, but He wasn't necessarily angry or sorrowful over the same things we would be.

Jesus was troubled, not for himself, but for another. Specifically, He was troubled for the very one who was going to deliver Him up to a cruel death. He was troubled over the soul who would betray Him.

While the disciples didn't yet know Judas was the betrayer, they understood the force of Jesus' words: there was a traitor in their midst. To their credit, they looked at one another and asked, "Is it me?" (see Mark 14:19).

Jesus was showing that He knew exactly what Judas was up to.

If Judas' true colors were as obvious as some may think, they would have all pointed to him at once: "It's the guy in the black robe, isn't it, Lord?"

But John, who always stayed close to Jesus, was given the assignment to find out:

> Now there was leaning on Jesus' bosom one of His disciples, whom Jesus loved. Simon Peter therefore motioned to him to ask who it was of whom He spoke. Then, leaning back on Jesus' breast, he said to Him, "Lord, who is it?" Jesus answered, "It is he to whom I shall give a piece of bread when I have dipped it."

> And having dipped the bread, He gave it to
> Judas Iscariot, the son of Simon. (vv. 23–26)

Judas was sitting at the left hand of Jesus, the place of honor. No doubt the Lord had invited him to come and sit with Him on this particular night. In that culture, when someone would take a piece of unleavened bread, dip it into a common dish, and offer it to another, it was a gesture of friendship, trust, and closeness. And that is what Jesus did for Judas. To offer this food to Judas was an act of friendship. It was an act of fellowship. It was an act of mercy. And it was an offer of forgiveness. Jesus was reaching out to Judas, as if to say, "Old friend, we have walked a lot of roads together. You don't have to go through with this. You don't have to betray me. Here is my friendship. I still offer it to you. All you have to do is take it." Jesus was showing that He knew exactly what Judas was up to. He was also demonstrating His love to the very end. But Judas slammed the door in Jesus' face:

> And having dipped the bread, He gave it to
> Judas Iscariot, the son of Simon. Now after
> the piece of bread, Satan entered him. Then
> Jesus said to him, "What you do, do quickly."
> (vv . 26–27)

In spite of Judas' willful and deliberate wickedness, Jesus continued to offer him the opportunity to repent and not go through with his plan. In fact, Jesus offered Judas opportunity after opportunity to repent. But in Iscariot we see a clear pattern of the deception of sin, even in the most knowledgeable people. When He was in the Garden of Gethsemane and Judas arrived on the scene with the temple guard to arrest Him, Jesus asked, "Friend, why have you come?" (Matt. 26:50). Note how He called this betrayer "friend." And note how Judas betrayed Him with a kiss. He could have just pointed and said, "There's Jesus. He's the one you want. I'm out of here. I don't want to be a part of this." But he didn't. Instead, Judas kissed Him. In the original language, it could be translated to say that he kissed Jesus again and again. It wasn't just a peck on the cheek. Rather, it was a demonstration of affection. This made what Judas did all the more wicked.

Some have tried to paint Judas as a victim, even a pawn in the hand of God. But nothing could be further from the truth. He was wicked. Jesus would later refer to him as "the son of perdition" (John 17:12). Every step of the way, Judas was complicit in his betrayal of Jesus, falling increasingly under the power of the devil, culminating in actual possession by Satan himself (v. 27). And if ever Satan had a son, it was Judas. The only one who ever will equal and surpass Judas in wickedness will be the Antichrist.

In Judas we see a clear pattern of the deception of sin, even in the most knowledgeable people.

It's worth noting that Judas had been so effective in his lie, so cunning, and so skillful as an actor, that no one suspected him until Jesus made it very clear that he was the one. Judas had fooled everyone…except Jesus.

THE ULTIMATE EXAMPLE

There is a lesson to be learned from Judas' life. In many ways, it is incomprehensible that a man who had such an opportunity could so squander it. Think about it: Judas spent every waking hour walking and talking with God incarnate. What an incredible privilege that was. Unbelievers often will say that it's the hypocrisy of Christians that keeps them away from Christianity. But that is nothing more than an excuse, really. Case in point: the example of Jesus in contrast to the actions of Judas.

Judas had fooled everyone...except Jesus.

Jesus was the ultimate example, to say the least. He never did a single, inconsistent thing. He never lost His temper, never said an unkind thing, and never told a lie. He never had a single thought out of harmony with His father. He was the perfect, flawless example. Yet Judas not only refused to believe, but he also turned against Jesus, selling him out for thirty pieces of silver—a price commonly paid in those days to purchase a slave.

It is amazing to consider that Judas was even one of the original Twelve. Keep in mind that he had been chosen by Jesus himself. Still, the foreknowledge of God does not change the responsibility of man. Even though Jesus already knew what would take place, Judas, of his own choosing, deliberately betrayed the Lord. This was in spite of the fact that Judas had personally heard the great teachings of Jesus. He had listened as Jesus delivered the Sermon on the Mount, heard firsthand the story of the Prodigal Son, and had been privy to the Olivet Discourse. He had personally heard Jesus' words and teachings on hypocrisy and His warning about the wheat and the tares. He had personally witnessed some big-time miracles, such as the Feeding of the Five Thousand, the blind receiving their sight, and the resurrection of Lazarus from the dead. With his own ears, he heard Jesus say, "Not everyone who says to Me, 'Lord, Lord,' shall enter the kingdom of heaven, but he who does the will of My Father in heaven" (Matt. 7:21). He had countless opportunities to believe. And like Pharaoh in Moses' day, the more he saw, the harder his heart became.

It reminds me of Saul, a man who had been blessed and called by God to be the first king of Israel. He began well, but small compromises led to larger ones, until God rejected him as Israel's king. When an evil spirit began to plague him, a young shepherd named David was called in to sing and worship the Lord before the tormented king, which would bring temporary relief. But not long after David left, the tormenting spirit would

return. So why didn't Saul turn to God, who could
have brought him help? Because he was filled
with anger, jealousy, and wickedness. And he just
got worse and worse.

In the same way, some unbelievers will come
to church for some "relief." The worship music and
teaching of God's Word bring them a measure of
comfort, but then they continue to live in sin, with
no desire to change. They think worship, Bible
study, or even Communion will do them some good.
And it will—if they follow the Lord. But if they do
not, it could actually do them harm. The apostle
Paul warned against receiving the elements of
Communion without knowing and following the
God those elements represent:

> For he who eats and drinks in an unworthy
> manner eats and drinks judgment to himself,
> not discerning the Lord's body. For this
> reason many are weak and sick among you,
> and many sleep. For if we would judge
> ourselves, we would not be judged. (1 Cor.
> 11:29–31)

The same sun that softens the wax hardens the
clay. The same sun that makes a living tree grow
makes a dead tree dry up. And the same gospel
message that transforms one life drives another

deeper into sin, if he or she doesn't respond in the appropriate way. It is really frightening that someone could be exposed to so much truth and yet remain in, even be strengthened in, unbelief. If a person can habitually commit sin without any sense of conviction or remorse, that would be a clear indicator that he or she does not know God.

The foreknowledge of God does not change the responsibility of man.

WHEN GUILT IS GOOD

The point is that people are missing the point if they go to church for a little relief. It is more than that. It is walking with God. The true child of God, though still a sinner, will not live in a pattern of sin. As 1 John 3:9–10 tells us,

> Those who have been born into God's family do not sin, because God's life is in them. So they can't keep on sinning, because they have been born of God. So now we can tell who are children of God and who are children of the Devil. Anyone who does not obey God's commands and

does not love other Christians does not
belong to God. (NLT)

❧

He had countless opportunities to believe.

❧

If you find yourself under immediate conviction
when you start to cross a line you know you
shouldn't, if you find that deep guilt sets in when
you have sinned, then rejoice. Why? Because it
proves that you are indeed a child of God. If one
of my sons does something wrong, it is my right,
even my responsibility, as his father to correct
and even discipline him if necessary. That is not
my right with someone else's child (though I wish
it were at times). The same is true of God. He
convicts and disciplines those who are His.
The writer of Hebrews reminds us,

> And you have forgotten that word of
> encouragement that addresses you as
> sons: "My son, do not make light of the
> Lord's discipline, and do not lose heart
> when he rebukes you, because the Lord
> disciplines those he loves, and he punishes
> everyone he accepts as a son." Endure
> hardship as discipline; God is treating you
> as sons. For what son is not disciplined by

his father? If you are not disciplined (and
everyone undergoes discipline), then you
are illegitimate children and not true sons.
(Heb. 12:5–8 NIV)

Judas was able to do the wicked things he
did because he really never knew Jesus. Sure,
he knew *about* Him more than most people,
but he never *knew* Him. His life could be
summed up in the phrase from Luke's account
of these tragic circumstances: "So he went his
way…" (Luke 22:4). As Proverbs tells us, "There
is a way that seems right to a man, but its end is
the way of death" (14:12).

Judas was not walking with God. He was
exposed to all that truth, yet his heart became
irreparably hardened. So Jesus told him, "What
you are about to do, do quickly" (v. 27 NIV). And
Judas left.

THE PURPOSE OF COMMUNION

I would imagine the mood in that room changed
dramatically. With Judas gone, the Passover would
continue. Jesus and His disciples could have their
first Communion together. Communion is a place
for believers, after all, not pretenders or betrayers.

It is a family celebration and gathering, a time to look long and hard at a number of things.

First, we are to look at Jesus. Luke 22:19 says, "And He took bread, gave thanks and broke it, and gave it to them, saying, 'This is My body which is given for you; do this in remembrance of Me.'" Jesus was saying, "Remember Me. Don't forget Me or what I did for you."

The true child of God, though still a sinner, will not live in a pattern of sin.

Second, we are to look to Jesus at the cross. As 1 Corinthians 11:26 says, "For as often as you eat this bread and drink this cup, you proclaim the Lord's death till He comes." At the Communion table, we are to look back to Calvary where our salvation was purchased. There, we are reminded of the words of Jesus, who said, "It is finished!" No longer are we to look rituals, religion, rites, or even good works to save us. Our personal salvation is a gift to us from God, purchased with the blood of Jesus. Jesus wants us to remember the offensive, bloody, unsophisticated, blessed cross, so we don't start believing that our salvation was the result

of our own strength. Jesus wants us to remember
how our salvation was purchased. He wants us
to remember Calvary, His broken body, and His
shed blood for us.

Third, we are to look inside. The Bible says, "A
man ought to examine himself before he eats of the
bread and drinks of the cup" (1 Cor. 11:28 NIV).
We are to ask the Holy Spirit to reveal anything
in our hearts that might get in the way of our
fellowship with God and others. It may be an
unconfessed sin or a wrong attitude we have been
nursing, such as being prideful, ungrateful, or
judgmental. Our attitude should reflect that of the
psalmist, who said, "Search me, O God, and know
my heart; test me and know my thoughts. Point
out anything in me that offends you, and lead me
along the path of everlasting life" (Ps. 119:23–24
NLT). Essentially, we should say, "Lord, if there is
something here in my heart that is wrong, please
show me what it is."

Fourth, we are to look to other believers. In
speaking of Communion, the apostle Paul said,
"And we all eat from one loaf, showing that we are
one body" (1 Cor. 10:17 NLT). Christianity isn't a
solo experience. We are to encourage one another,

bless one another, and correct one another. As Romans 12 says, "So in Christ we who are many form one body, and each member belongs to all the others. We have different gifts, according to the grace given us. … Be devoted to one another in brotherly love. Honor one another above yourselves" (vv. 5–6, 10 NIV). So when we take part in Communion, we do so as a body, as a family, and as friends. This is even more important as we come closer to Christ's return. Hebrews 10:25 reminds us, "Let us not give up meeting together, as some are in the habit of doing, but let us encourage one another—and all the more as you see the Day approaching" (NIV).

Jesus wants us to remember how our salvation was purchased.

Fifth, we are to look forward to Christ's return. Jesus instituted a reminder, not a mere ritual. The primary purpose of Communion is to remember Jesus: "For as often as you eat this bread and drink this cup, you proclaim the Lord's death till He comes" (1 Corinthians 11:26). He gave us this ceremony, if you will, to jog our memories.

Just as my wedding ring serves as a reminder that I am married, the Communion service reminds me to remember Jesus.

Christianity isn't a solo experience.

But what does it actually mean to remember Jesus? It means to revisit the cross in your imagination, remembering His suffering, His sacrifice, and the nails in His hands and feet.

It also means to remember that He is coming back again. Communion reminds us that He came—and that He is coming again. Sometimes we live as though Jesus never came to this earth, or we behave as though He is not coming back again. But He is. Are you ready for His return?

GOD'S CURE FOR HEART TROUBLE

John 14:1–6

Have you ever felt stressed-out to the max, when it seemed like everything went wrong all at once? And then, when it seemed it couldn't get any worse, it did? Or let me put it another way: Have you ever driven on a crowded freeway at rush hour?

One of the downsides of our Information Age with cell phones, PDAs, Blackberries, Treos, and even watches that can give us sports scores, the weather, and the latest news is that we are barraged by information. As a result, we have even *more* to be worried and stressed-out about. That is why I think this also could be called the Stress Age.

It's funny how when we are young, we are stressed out about getting older. We wonder about things like, "What will I do for a living?"; "Where am I going to go to college?"; "Who am I going to marry?" And then, when we are older, we wish we were younger again. We have reached some of our goals, but we think to ourselves, "When I was younger, it was so much better. Those were the days. There was no stress back then."

AT THE SOURCE OF OUR HEART TROUBLE

But the reality is that we will have stress in our lives no matter what stage of life we are in. A survey of adults and their teenaged children was conducted in which they were asked what stresses them out. The number-one thing that stressed out the parents was fighting with their kids. And the number-one thing that stressed out teenagers was fighting with their parents.

―――――――

Worrying does not empty tomorrow of its sorrow; it empties today of its strength.

―――――――

The second-most stressful thing for parents was getting their teenagers to study. And what was the second most stressful thing for teenagers? Doing their homework.

The next most stressful thing for the parents was the teenagers themselves. For the teenagers, the next most stressful thing for them was their parents.

Then the parents said they were stressed
out by how to *get* skinny. The teenagers, in turn,
were stressed out about how to *stay* skinny.

Further, parents were stressed about
promotions and raises, while their teenagers
were stressed about grades.

Parents were stressed out by chaos and
noise, but the teenagers were stressed out by
peace and quiet.

Finally, parents were stressed-out by work,
and teenagers were stressed-out by chores.
So we all have things that stress us.

But stress can be serious stuff. Studies suggest
that high levels of stress lead to a number of
health problems, including obesity, heart attacks,
ulcers, depression, nervous breakdowns, and even
cancer. And the Centers for Disease Control and
Prevention says that in the USA, up to 90 percent
of visits to physicians may be trigged by stress-
related illnesses.[1]

Maybe your life is filled with intense stress
right now. Without a doubt, life certainly is filled
with troubles. As the Book of Job tells us, "Man
is born to trouble, as the sparks fly upward"
(Job 5:7). There are health troubles, family

troubles, boyfriend and girlfriend troubles, and financial troubles. Surveys have indicated that 70 percent of American moms find motherhood "incredibly stressful," while 30 percent of mothers of young children suffer from depression.[2]

They were afraid that even though they might escape death, they would have to go on living without Jesus.

Disappointment is also a source of trouble in our lives, and we encounter many disappointments. We are disappointed with ourselves, because we are not always what we want to be. We want to be strong, but we are weak. We want to be successful, but we experience many failures. We want to be loved, but people often are indifferent toward us.

Circumstances also bring trouble, such as the loss of a job, sickness, and even uncertainty about the future. And in our post-9/11 world, there are fears that we all have as Americans. The nuclear fears from the Cold War-era apparently haven't disappeared, even though the Soviet Union is gone. According to one article, "Most Americans think nuclear weapons are so dangerous that no country should have them, and a majority believes it's likely that terrorists or a nation will use them within five years."[4] The article also cites an AP-Ipsos poll in which 53 percent of Americans surveyed said they thought "a nuclear attack by one country against another is somewhat or very likely by 2010."[5]

THE PROBLEM WITH WORRY

Without a doubt, we're living in stressful times. But worrying does not empty tomorrow of its sorrow; it empties today of its strength. God will give us the strength to face each day with enough grace to manage. Whatever you may face, He will not abandon you in your hour of need. But if you worry about your circumstances, you only will compound your troubles.

An old fable teaches a valuable lesson about this. Death was walking toward a town one morning when a man stopped and asked, "What are you intending to do?"

"I plan on taking one hundred people," Death replied.

"That's horrible!" the man exclaimed.

"That's what I do. It's just the way it is," Death told him.

The man hurried ahead of Death into town to warn everyone about what was coming. As evening fell, he met Death again. The man protested, "You told me you were going to take only one hundred people. Why did a thousand die?"

"I kept my word," Death responded. "I took only one hundred people. Worry took the others."

Many of the people in American hospital beds today are constant worriers. Studies have shown that 43 percent of all adults have their health affected because of worry and stress, and 75 to 90 percent of all visits to primary care physicians are stress-related.[3] Obviously, we're a culture in the constant grip of anxiety and worry. Written on countless American gravestones could be the epitaph, "Hurried, worried, buried."

Maybe we should consider hiring someone to worry for us, like one man who was known to be a real worrywart. He was always fretting about something. But one day, his friend was surprised to see him looking completely relaxed and at ease, seemingly without a care in the world. His friend commented that he didn't seem to be uptight.

"I haven't worried for a good month," the man replied with a smile.

"Really? Why?"

"Simple. I hired someone to worry for me," he said.

"You what?" his friend asked, amazed. "Where did you find somebody like that?"

"I took out an ad in the paper," he said.

"You did? What did the ad say?" his friend asked.

"I will pay you one thousand dollars a day if you come and worry for me."

Stress is a normal human response to changes and problems in our lives.

"A thousand dollars a day? You don't make anything close to that kind of money. How do you intend to pay this guy?"

"That's for him to worry about," the man replied.

THREE CURES FOR HEART TROUBLE

I'm thankful the Bible is a practical book that speaks to our lives and tells us how to deal with issues like stress, agitation, fear of the unknown, and much more. And that brings us to Jesus' words to stressed-out, agitated people. These words offer help to hearts that are disturbed. They are God's cure for heart trouble:

> Let not your heart be troubled; you believe in God, believe also in Me. In My Father's house are many mansions; if it were not so, I would have told you. I go to prepare a place for you. And if I go and prepare a place for you, I will come again and receive you to Myself; that where I am, there you may be also. (John 14:1–3)

The word that Jesus used for "troubled" could be translated, "agitated, disturbed, or thrown into confusion." It is a picturesque word. The idea behind it is, "Don't let your heart shudder." Interestingly, it was the same word used in John 13:21 to describe Jesus' emotions as Judas went astray.

It is also a strong word, and Jesus was specifically saying to the disciples, in light of the imminent cross, "It may look like your world is falling apart and that darkness will overtake you, but don't let your hearts be troubled!"

Notice Jesus didn't say, "Mull over your problems." Rather, He said, "Don't be troubled." In other words, He was showing them that

although there was cause to be troubled, there
was even greater cause *not* to be. Regardless
of what may cause us to be troubled, as Christians,
there is more cause *not* to be troubled. Jesus laid
out for the disciples (and us) three reasons why.

---

*We must read and believe
what God's Word says to us,
and then we must trust Him.*

First, we can take God at His word. "You
believe in God," Jesus said. "Believe also in Me"
(v. 1). In the original language, this is a command.
The disciples had just received some unnerving
news from Jesus in the Upper Room. He told them
that one of them would betray Him. Then He told
Peter that he would deny Him three times. But
self-confident Peter was certain that not only could
he follow his Lord, but he could also die with Him
and for Him. Poor Peter. He didn't know his own
heart. Nor do we know our own hearts, except
for one thing: our hearts can be easily troubled.

The heaviest blow of all was the fact that Jesus
was going to leave them. Their whole world came
crashing down in a moment's time. They were in a

state of panic. What would happen to them? What about the future? And if someone as devoted as the outspoken Peter would deny the Lord, what about the rest of them? Would they, too, fall away? Jesus knew they were afraid—afraid of what was coming. They were afraid of death, afraid that they, along with Jesus, were going to be executed by the Jews. They knew of the opposition that had developed against them in Jerusalem, the bitter hatred of the Pharisees, and their determination to eliminate Jesus and all His disciples. They knew they were in danger. So their hearts were deeply troubled as they were gathered together with Jesus.

Whatever your circumstances or hardship, believe that He has a purpose in those circumstances.

But more than recognizing the potential physical danger to themselves, they were aware of His words about leaving them. This struck abject terror in their hearts. They were afraid that even though they might escape death, they would have to go on living without Jesus. And it was a fate worse than death to be without Jesus. They could bear to die with Him, but they could not bear to live or die *without* Him.

So as Jesus was there with them, He spoke these words of reassurance: "Let not your heart be troubled." Does this mean that Christians never should feel anxious, pressured, or afraid? Does this mean such feelings are sinful? Are we supposed to feel cheerful and confident all the time? Some have taken John 14 and other passages out of context to imply this.

But that is not what the Bible teaches. Several times in this and the other three Gospels, we read that Jesus was "deeply troubled in Spirit." So, from the example of Jesus, we cannot expect to be stress-free all the time. Stress is a normal human response to changes and problems in our lives. When Jesus said, "Let not your heart be troubled," He was not saying we would not be stressed or troubled by life. He was saying there is a way to overcome it.

What is amazing is that He made this statement to begin with. There He was, ready to embark on the journey to the cruel cross of Calvary. The stress, agitation, and pressure that would be placed on Him would be unsurpassed. No one would ever suffer as He soon would suffer. Yet to His disciples,

He said, "Let not your heart be troubled. ..." They could not experience His feelings, but He could experience theirs. So He said, "Believe in Me" (v. 1). In the original Greek, this is not only a command, but a *double command*. There was force behind His words, as though Jesus were saying, "Your agitation is a result of not believing what God has said in the Scriptures concerning My death and resurrection." The disciples knew Jesus, and they had every reason to trust Him. He had never let them down. But they didn't have the "big picture" of the crucifixion and resurrection. Did Jesus know what He was doing? Yes. Could He be trusted? Absolutely!

In the same way, Jesus sees the "big picture" with us as well. We must remember that Jesus was not only speaking to these troubled disciples two thousand years ago, but to us as well. We tend to think on the short-term, with a limited view of things. We think of the temporal, while God thinks of the eternal. We think of today, while God is planning for tomorrow. We think of our comfort, while God thinks of our character. We think of the path of least resistance, while God thinks of the paths of righteousness.

Our stress and agitation and troubled hearts come from ignoring His Word. Or it may be due to a simple lack of reading it to begin with. But the only way we will be able to bring God's Word into our lives is by taking the time to read it and think about it and meditate on it.

We all have a longing for heaven, whether we know it or not.

Let's say that you are having a problem with your computer. What are you going to do? Are you going to hope that somehow Bill Gates senses your stress, picks up the phone, and calls you to tell you what to do? Or do you think that Bill Gates will speak to your heart in this set of circumstances? No, he won't be dong that. Instead, the company he founded known as Microsoft gave you something called a user's manual that you need to open and carefully read.

God certainly can speak to our hearts, but the primary way He speaks to us is through His user's manual, the Bible. Joshua 1:8 says, "Study this Book of the Law continually. Meditate on it day and night so you may be sure to obey all that is written in it. Only then will you succeed" (NLT).

Or, we may have read God's Word, but we have failed to believe it or act on it. James tells us, "For if you just listen and don't obey, it is like looking at your face in a mirror but doing nothing to improve your appearance. You see yourself, walk away, and forget what you look like" (James 1:23– 24 NLT). We must read and believe what God's Word says to us, and then we must trust Him.

There is only one thing that God cannot do, and that is lie.

Whatever your circumstances or hardship, believe that He has a purpose in those circumstances: "And we know that all things work together for good to those who love God, to those who are the called according to His purpose" (Romans 8:28).

Second, our hearts should not be troubled because we are going to heaven. Jesus said, "In My Father's house are many mansions ..." (v. 2). No matter what happens to you on this earth, it pales when compared with this great hope. The words of the apostle Paul remind us of this truth:

For our present troubles are quite small and won't last very long. Yet they produce for us an immeasurably great glory that will last forever! So we don't look at the troubles we can see right now; rather, we look forward to what we have not yet seen. For the troubles we see will soon be over, but the joys to come will last forever. (2 Cor. 4:17–18 NLT)

Deep inside, we all long for this place we have never been. In his book, *The Problem of Pain*, C. S. Lewis calls this the inconsolable longing, "the secret signature of each soul, the incommunicable and unappeasable want. ..."[6] We all have a longing for heaven, whether we know it or not. And heaven is waiting for the child of God. You have His Word on it. There is only one thing that God *cannot* do, and that is lie.

Jesus has gone to prepare a place for us, and that is a key element of our comfort. When you are expecting a guest in your home, you prepare the room ahead of time. You might know this guest likes certain books or treats, so you customize the room. That way, when your guest arrives, he or she will feel at home. What are your likes? Do you favor modern architecture? Your new home will surpass anything that Frank Lloyd Wright ever envisioned. Do you like classic country? Ralph Lauren could not touch what God has prepared for you. Whatever the case, heaven will be great, to say the least.

When we read these words of Jesus, we often envision beautiful, palatial mansions like we might see in a place like Beverly Hills. We might be in for a surprise, however, like the well-known minister and the New York cab driver who both died and went to heaven. Simon Peter met them at the Pearly Gates. Approaching the cab driver first, Peter introduced himself and said, "I'm in charge of housing here. I want to direct you to the place we have set up for you." He put his hand on the cabby's shoulder and pointed into the distance. "You see that mansion over there on that beautiful, green hilltop? That's yours, my friend. Go and enjoy it."

Whatever you may face, He will not abandon you in your hour of need.

The cab driver smiled, tipped his hat, and walked off with a spring in his step toward his new estate.

At the sight of this, the minister stood a little taller. He thought, "If a New York cabby gets a mansion like that, imagine what I will get!"

Peter called the minister forward and said, "See that beat-up shack down there in the valley? That is your place. You go there."

Shocked, the minister said, "Excuse me, Peter. I'm a man of God. I've spent my life in the ministry, serving the Lord and preaching the gospel. I don't understand how a New York cab driver would get a mansion while I just get a shack in the valley!"

"Here's what it comes down to," Peter replied. "It seems that when you preached, people slept. But when he drove, people prayed."

But I think the "dwelling places" Jesus spoke of probably refers to the new bodies we will receive. We're offered a preview in 2 Corinthians 5:1–2:

> For we know that when this earthly tent we live in is taken down—when we die and leave these bodies—we will have a home in heaven, an eternal body made for us by God himself and not by human hands. We grow weary in our present bodies, and we long for the day when we will put on our heavenly bodies like new clothing. (NLT)

The Bible doesn't tell us a lot about heaven, probably because it is so far beyond our comprehension. It would be like taking a little three-month-old baby, propping him up with pillows, and saying to him, "Now I am going to tell you about Hawaii. Are you ready?" You get out a big book with gorgeous photos of Hawaii. "Look. This is the island of Maui. See how nice it is?" The baby is just going to sit there, because he doesn't have the capacity to comprehend the information you are conveying to him.

In the same way, as God speaks of the glories of heaven, there is no way, in this life at least, that we can fully grasp it. Even the apostle Paul, who personally caught a glimpse of it, said, "But I do know that I was caught up into paradise and heard things so astounding that they cannot be told" (2 Cor. 12:3–4 NLT).

Jesus is preparing wonderful homes for each of us, and that is a comfort. Some may label this as pie-in-the-sky escapism, claiming that people who think this way are "so heavenly minded, they are no earthly good." But I don't believe that it's possible for us to be so heavenly minded that we are no earthly good. The reality of our future heavenly

home helps through the trials of this life.
And the fact of the matters is that when we
truly are heavenly minded, we are the greatest
earthly good.

Those who have done the most for this world
have usually thought more of the next one. Any
honest look at history will reveal that it has always
been committed Christians who have let their
lights shine (see Matt. 5:16). They have been
the ones who have started the universities, built
shelters and hospitals, and have gone into the war-
torn and famine-ridden areas of the world with
food, medicine, and clothing. I've heard of a lot
of church-affiliated hospitals, but personally, I've
never heard of an atheist hospital. It is indeed those
who are heavenly minded who have done the most
earthly good.

*He will return for those who
are watching and waiting.*

*Third, our hearts should not be troubled
because Jesus will come again.* He told the
disciples, "And if I go and prepare a place for you,
I will come again and receive you to Myself; that

where I am, there you may be also" (v. 3). In our fallen world, we find relief for our troubled hearts from the fact that Jesus is coming back to receive us to himself.

When General Douglas McArthur left the Philippines in the early months of World War II, he fled Corregidor in apparent defeat. Upon reaching Australia, he sent back the now-famous declaration to the people of the Philippines: "I shall return." It took him a little bit of time, but he kept his promise. Three years later, General McArthur returned, stood on Philippine soil, and made his second historic statement: "I have returned."

Those who have done the most for this world have usually thought more of the next one.

In the same way our Lord has said to us, "I will come again." And some day, in the not-too-distant future, He will set His foot back on Planet Earth and say, "I have returned!" And it may be sooner than we think. The Lord will not merely send for us, but will come in person to escort us to the Father's house:

For the Lord Himself will descend from
heaven with a shout, with the voice of an
archangel, and with the trumpet of God.
And the dead in Christ will rise first. Then
we who are alive and remain shall be caught
up together with them in the clouds to meet
the Lord in the air. And thus we shall always
be with the Lord. Therefore comfort one
another with these words. (1 Thess. 4:16–18)

Notice Jesus' choice of words when He spoke
about His return. He did not say, "I will come again
and *take* you to Myself," but said, "I will come
again and *receive* you to Myself" (v. 3, emphasis
mine). It is not something He will do against our
will. He will return for those who are watching
and waiting.

JUST ONE WAY

Jesus then offered a somewhat mysterious
statement, perhaps to elicit a response from the
disciples: "And where I go you know, and the way
you know" (v. 4). Yet Thomas was the only one bold
enough to ask Jesus what He meant. Thomas has
been given the title, "Doubting Thomas," but he
was more of a skeptic, really. The doubter doubts,
even when the facts are clear. But the skeptic

looks carefully, wanting to see for himself. Thomas wasn't one to let others do his thinking for him. He was behaving more like "Honest Thomas" than "Doubting Thomas." He didn't understand and said so: "Lord, we do not know where You are going, and how can we know the way?" (v. 4).

It seems to me the disciples would act as though they understood something Jesus was telling them, when, in fact, they did not. Thomas was honest enough to speak out and say, "Lord, we don't know where You are going." Aren't you glad Thomas said that? Jesus didn't rebuke him, but instead used Thomas' question as an opportunity to expand His revelation of himself. And His reply to Thomas is one of the most famous and profound statements in all of Scripture: "Jesus said to him, 'I am the way, the truth, and the life. No one comes to the Father except through Me'" (v. 6).

In that final day, the big question from God to you will be, "What did you do with My Son, Jesus Christ?"

This statement also is one of, if not the most, controversial aspects of our faith. By believing this, we are saying that Jesus Christ is the only way to God. This is hard for some people to accept. They choke on this, arguing that Christians are narrow-minded. "How dare you suggest that your faith is the only true faith?" they say. "How dare you say that all religions are not true and that all roads do not lead to God?"

The only reason I say it is because Jesus said it. And if I offer anything less or anything more than this, then I am not offering the true gospel message. The Bible says, "Nor is there salvation in any other, for there is no other name under heaven given among men by which we must be saved" (Acts 4:12), and "There is one God and one Mediator between God and men, the Man Christ Jesus" (1 Tim. 2:5). It also says, "Not by works of righteousness which we have done, but according to His mercy He saved us ..." (Titus 3:5). Jesus said He was the way, the truth, and the life. No one comes to the Father except through Him. It's as simple as that.

If you believe the words of Jesus himself, and think and act biblically, then you must believe that Jesus Christ and His finished work on the cross (and not human effort) is the basis on which you will get to heaven.

On the cross, Jesus said, "It is finished!" He
didn't say, "It is still in process." God has already
done this work for you. So the moment you
acknowledge Jesus as your Savior, you are saying
you believe He died on the cross for you and paid
the price for your sins. It means you have turned
from that sin and are putting your faith in Him. It
means you have become a child of God and have a
guaranteed residence waiting for you on the other
side in heaven. And it means when Christ comes
back again, if it happens in your lifetime, He will
take you with Him. It is belief in Jesus—and Jesus
alone—that will save you. Period. It is not that plus
your good works.

But let me add that although good works won't
save you, they are good evidence that you are
saved. So if you have really embraced Christ as
Savior and Lord, it will affect the way that you want
to live. You will want to do what the Bible says. You
will want to go to church. You will want to study the
Bible. You will want to pray. You will want to do all
of the things the Bible tells you should do as a true
follower of Christ. But those things don't save you.
Rather, they are a result of your salvation.

So let me ask you, do you have heart trouble today? Are you agitated, stressed out, or under pressure? Then remember God's cure for heart trouble:

1. His Word is true.
2. We are going to heaven.
3. He is coming back for us.

These are promises given only to the believer, the child of God who has put his or her faith in Jesus Christ. If you are not a believer, then sadly, none of this applies to you.

The reality of our future heavenly home helps through the trials of this life.

And if you are not a believer, you ought to be agitated. You ought to be stressed out. You ought to be very concerned, most significantly about your soul and what will happen to you when you die. Because in that final day, the big question from God to you will be, "What did you do with My Son, Jesus Christ?" It won't so much be the sin question as much as it will be the *Son* question, because there is no other name given under heaven by which we can be saved.

Jesus can give this hope of heaven to you right now, along with the forgiveness of your sins and the assurance that if He comes in our lifetime, you will be ready to meet Him. Do you have that assurance? Jesus died on the cross. He shed His blood for our sins. He rose again from the dead. And not only that, but He is standing at the door of your life and knocking. If you will hear His voice and open the door, He will come in.

You can start today and see God's cure for heart trouble at work in your life.

3 THE SECRET TO SPIRITUAL GROWTH

John 15

I read the story of a father who was taking his daughter to her first day of middle school, and he decided he should start talking to her about some serious stuff, like the meaning of life.

Her response was, "My meaning of life is to please Mom!"

You were created to know God.

"Well, what about Dad?" he asked.

"Your meaning of life is to please Mom too!"

But what is the meaning of life, really? As the great theologian, Forrest Gump, said, "Life is like a box of chocolates. You never know what you're gonna get." Forrest also said, "Mama always told me that dying was a part of life." And of course, "Stupid is as stupid does."

Hopefully, there is more to life than what Forrest's theology covers, because life passes by so quickly. Sometimes events will occur in our lives that get our attention, things that we might refer to as divine wake-up calls. It could be a close brush with death, the break-up of a marriage, or the death of a loved one. It's something that gets you back to asking yourself the question, "What am I doing with my life?"

THE MEANING OF LIFE

So many are searching for meaning in life. Consider the incredible success of Rick Warren's book, *The Purpose Driven Life*. It has been the top bestselling non-fiction book, after the Bible, in publishing history!

If you aim at nothing, you're bound to hit it.

Dr. Hugh Moorehead, a philosophy professor at Northeastern Illinois University, once wrote to 250 of the best-known philosophers, scientists, writers, and intellectuals in the world, asking them, "What is the meaning of life?" He then published their responses in a book. Some offered their best guesses. Some admitted they just made up a purpose for life. Others were honest enough to say they were clueless.

Clearly we need to know where we are going in life and why. We need to know what our goals and objectives are, because, as it's been said, "If you aim at nothing, you're bound to hit it." What have you been aiming at in life? If you have no goals, no purpose, and no guiding principles, you will waste your life. What are your goals? These are things that every person should be asking, because they are of the greatest importance.

Younger people who are looking ahead in life definitely should be asking these questions, because life goes by so quickly. Someone has described the four stages of life this way:

1. You believe in Santa Claus.
2. You don't believe in Santa Claus.
3. You are Santa Claus.
4. You look like Santa Claus.

WHY WE EXIST

So why do we exist? Jesus answered this question for us: You were created to know God. Well-known atheist Bertrand Russell said, "Unless you assume a God, the question of life's purpose is meaningless."

The Bible tells us this as well. Creation, including humanity, was made subject to futility, or with a built-in emptiness. Romans 8:20 tells us, "For the creation was subjected to futility, not willingly, but because of Him who subjected it in hope...." Or as another translation reads, "Subject to emptiness."

After Adam's sin, God said, "Cursed is the ground for your sake; in toil you shall eat of it all the days of your life" (Gen. 3:17). That is why if you are seeking fulfillment, purpose, or meaning from this world in and of itself, you won't find it. God created it in such a way that it was lacking, so that we would turn to Him. Solomon said, "Then I looked on all the works that my hands had done and on the labor in which I had toiled; and indeed all was vanity and grasping for the wind ... " (Eccl. 2:11). You were created with a God-shaped blank in your life so that you will seek to know Him. The Bible tells us that "[God] created all things, and by [His] will they exist and were created" (Rev. 4:11).

Awhile back, I attended two funeral services, both for faithful followers of Jesus Christ who died in their early seventies. One was for a woman named Carmen who had dedicated her life to helping orphans in Mexico. The other was for a man named Perry, who was an usher at the church I pastor, Harvest Christian Fellowship. He worked tirelessly behind the scenes as a volunteer at our radio broadcast, *A New Beginning*, at Harvest Crusades, and on mission trips. And he did it all *after* he retired. Both Carmen and Perry lived their lives to glorify and honor God. And I have no doubt that God said to both of them, "Well done, good and faithful servant."

The worst tragedy is not a life cut short as much as it is a life wasted.

A long life isn't nearly as important as one that has purpose. We are all looking for and desiring meaning and purpose in life. And the worst tragedy is not a life cut short as much as it is a life wasted. In 1948, Jim Elliot wrote in his journal, "I seek not a long life, but a full one, like You, Lord Jesus." Ten years later, as a missionary to Ecuador, he was martyred at the hands of the Waodani tribe he was attempting to reach with the gospel. Unlike Jim Elliot, some have lived long lives in terms of years, but it never could be said of them that they lived *full* lives.

Thousands of years ago, the prophet Daniel interpreted the writing on the wall for the rebellious Babylonian king, Belshazzar: "You have been weighed in the balances, and found wanting" (Dan. 5:27). Daniel provided the reason for Belshazzar's wasted life:

> You have lifted yourself up against the Lord of heaven. … And you have praised the gods of silver and gold, bronze and iron, wood and stone, which do not see or hear or know; and the God who holds your breath in His hand and owns all your ways, you have not glorified. (Dan. 5:23)

*Glorifying God and living a fruitful life …
this is why we are here.*

The root of his problem was that he failed to glorify God. We must not take it for granted, and we must never forget that God has given us the very breath of life.

WHAT WE WERE CHOSEN TO DO

So the first reason we exist is to glorify God. And the second reason is found here in John 15.

It is really an outgrowth of the first, which is to bear fruit: "You did not choose Me, but I chose you and appointed you that you should go and bear fruit, and that your fruit should remain, that whatever you ask the Father in My name He may give you" (v. 16). And again in verse 8, Jesus tells us this is how we glorify God: "By this My Father is glorified, that you bear much fruit; so you will be My disciples."

People will argue endlessly about how and why God chooses, or does not choose, people. But in doing so, they miss the forest for the trees. What is it that we were chosen to do? To go and bear fruit. This concept of "bearing fruit" is used often in Scripture to describe the results of someone who truly has a relationship with Jesus Christ. Jesus said, "You will know them by their fruits" (Matt. 7:16).

In the Parable of the Sower, Jesus said the seed that was sown on good ground bore fruit: "But these are the ones sown on good ground, those who hear the word, accept it, and bear fruit: some thirtyfold, some sixty, and some a hundred" (Mark 4:20). We were created to love and glorify God and to bear fruit.

Everything else is secondary. Career, success, and personal happiness are all secondary.

But what is fruit exactly? In John 15, Jesus answers this and a number of other significant questions, such as:

- How can I have a spiritually productive and fruitful life?

- How can I have overflowing joy in my life?

- How can I have answered prayers?

Abiding requires a continuing commitment.

The chapter opens with a metaphor in which Jesus says, "I am the true vine, and My Father is the vinedresser. Every branch in Me that does not bear fruit He takes away, and every branch that bears fruit He prunes, that it may bear more fruit" (vv. 1–2). A vine is intended to bear fruit. God intended Israel to bear fruit for Him to glorify His name before all the nations of the world. But He says, sadly, through the prophet Hosea, "Israel empties his vine; He brings forth fruit for himself" (Hosea 10:1). How this is true of so many today, even professing Christians. They are far more interested in what God can do for them than in what they can do for God. The Bible gives us this contrast between a life lived following the sinful nature and a life that bears spiritual fruit:

> When you follow the desires of your sinful nature, your lives will produce these evil results: Sexual immorality, impure thoughts, eagerness for lustful pleasure, idolatry, participation in demonic activities, hostility, quarreling, jealousy, outbursts of anger, selfish ambition, divisions, the feeling that everyone is wrong except those in your own little group, envy, drunkenness, wild parties, and others kinds of sin. Let me tell you again, as I have told you before, that anyone living that sort of life will not inherit the Kingdom of God. (Gal. 5:19–21 NLT)

———

We must learn to abide in Him.

———

What a perfect description it is of so many today: "lustful pleasure … impure thoughts … selfish ambitions … the feeling that everyone is wrong except those in your own little group." In contrast, the fruitful believer lives a life of peace and joy. "But when the Holy Spirit controls our lives, he will produce this kind of fruit in us: love joy, peace, patience, kindness, goodness, faithfulness, gentleness, and self-control … " (Gal. 5:22–23 NLT).

Abiding in Jesus takes time…and lots of it.

I heard about a little girl who was memorizing the list of the fruit of the Spirit: "love, joy, peace, patience, kindness, goodness, faithfulness, gentleness, and remote control. …" Is this what others see in your life? Or is the opposite true? If instead of love, there is hatred and bitterness; if instead of joy, there is gloom; if instead of peace, there is turmoil and guilt; if instead of gentleness, there is harshness and short tempter; if instead of faith, there is worry; if instead of meekness, there is pride and arrogance; and if instead of self-control, you find yourself a victim of your own passions, then either you don't know God at all, or you are living outside of fellowship with Him. In either case, a commitment or recommitment of your life to Christ would be in order.

HOW TO RECOGNIZE SPIRITUAL FRUIT

Glorifying God and living a fruitful life…this is why we are here. But what is this fruit that Jesus desires?

For one, living a godly and holy life is bearing fruit. As we see in Romans,

> And what was the result? It was not good, since now you are ashamed of the things you used to do, things that end in eternal doom. But now you are free from the power of sin and have become slaves of God. Now you can do those things that lead to holiness and result in eternal life. (Rom. 6:21–22 NLT)

Two, winning others to Jesus Christ and helping them to grow spiritually is fruit. The apostle Paul wrote to his friends at Rome, "I often planned to come to you … that I might have some fruit among you also, just as among the other Gentiles" (Rom. 1:13). And Proverbs tells us, "The fruit of the righteous is a tree of life, and he who wins souls is wise" (Prov. 11:30). Sometimes God gives us the privilege of personally leading someone to Christ. Other times, it simply means sowing a seed. But it is—and always will be—God who gives the increase. But certainly we have a part to play.

Three, sharing what God has blessed us with

is bearing fruit. When Paul collected an offering from the Gentiles for the poor saints in Jerusalem, he called that offering "fruit": "Therefore when I have performed this and have sealed to them this fruit, I shall go by way of you to Spain" (Rom. 15:28). When you invest financially in the work of God's kingdom, that is bearing fruit. Recognizing all we have comes from God, even our very breath, we happily give to see others come to Christ and grow in their faith. Again, Paul wrote, "Not that I seek the gift, but I seek the fruit that abounds to your account" (Phil. 4:17).

THE PREREQUISITE FOR BEARING FRUIT

I realize that all of this is a tall order: being holy, leading people to Christ, giving, serving ... so how do we bring forth this fruit Jesus desires? "Abide in Me, and I in you. As the branch cannot bear fruit of itself, unless it abides in the vine, neither can you, unless you abide in Me" (v. 4). To "abide" involves a permanence of position, not some flash-in-the-pan, try-God approach. Abiding requires a continuing commitment. Jesus said, "If anyone would come after me, he must deny himself and take up his cross *daily* and follow me" (Luke 9:23

NIV, emphasis mine). Abiding also means staying in a given place, thus providing lasting fruit.

The Christian life is not hard; it's impossible—without God's help.

Imagine planting a peach tree in your front yard and waiting for the fruit to grow. A week later, you get tired of waiting, so you dig it up and plant it in the backyard. The next week, you dig it up again and plant it again in the front yard. That tree will die, because it hasn't been able to take root. In the same way, there are people who make an alleged commitment to Christ, but they never take root. They go to church one week, then skip two. They read the Bible when they get around to it. They don't have any Christian friends. Yet abiding in Jesus takes time … and lots of it.

This can be hard for us to understand, because we live a mobile, fast-paced society. We just don't like to wait for things anymore. Here in Southern California where I live, we have special toll lanes called FastTraks that drivers can use. You have to buy a transmitter to take advantage of these lanes, but it gives you the privilege of often moving while others are stuck in gridlock. But there are no FastTraks on the narrow road that leads to life. We are still looking for the Cliffs Notes *Guide to Spirituality*. It takes a lot of time to become more like Jesus and bear fruit. The Bible speaks of slowing down, taking root, studying, denying, and obeying. What better way to spend your life than getting to know Him? If we want to grow spiritually and become more like Jesus, then we must learn to abide in Him.

We can be very busy,
in every way, without Christ.

HIS PART AND OURS

Here in John 15, Jesus described a two-sided process: His side and our side. We have a responsibility to remain in Jesus, and He has promised to remain with, and indeed live in, us. For a believer to be fruitful, both sides of this process must be operational. We should have no doubt that Jesus will hold up His end. But we must commit ourselves to keeping up our side. It is not enough for only one side to keep the agreement. It would be like getting married and breaking your wedding vows again and again. Then one day, your marriage falls apart, and you wonder why. A marriage cannot survive, or indeed flourish, with only one partner doing his or her part. So it is with our responsibility to remain in Jesus.

This means following Him each and every day, which consists of what we do and don't do. What we need to do is to stay as close as we can to Him, talking with Him daily, reading His Word, doing His will, obeying His commands, and worshipping Him. What we don't do is engage in practices that are sinful, even staying away from relationships and situations that might quench our thirst or dull our hunger for spiritual things. Yet some Christians think, "Oh, I don't need to concern myself with all of that! I'm strong, and I'll be fine!"

While discipline is necessary for bearing spiritual fruit, so is dependence.

My answer to them would be, "No, you are weak. And if you do not abide in Christ, then you will eventually fall."

The Christian life is not hard; it's impossible—
without God's help, that is. Jesus said, "I am the
vine, you are the branches. He who abides in Me,
and I in him, bears much fruit; for without Me you
can do nothing" (v. 5). Of course, this doesn't mean
things can't be done without Christ. A person could
still run a business without Christ, get married
and raise a family without Christ, go to church on
Sunday without Christ, and even preach sermons
without Christ. We can be very busy, in every way,
without Christ. It's like the bumper sticker I saw
that said, "Jesus is coming. Everyone look busy!"
Having said that, know this: If we have done it all
apart from Jesus, it ultimately will be fruitless.

―――

Nothing lies outside the reach
of prayer except that which lies
outside the will of God.

―――

You may have impressed hundreds, even thousands,
of people. But without God, it will have counted for
nothing. Yes, we want to be studying God's Word
and engaging in other vital Christian disciplines as
well. And while discipline is necessary for bearing
spiritual fruit, so is dependence.

One of the problems with fruit is that it takes so long to grow. So much so, you may not even be able to tell if there is all that much in your life. After all, if you were to sit down in front of a fruit tree and watch it, you wouldn't see anything happening. In the same way, spiritual fruit takes time to grow— lots of it.

EVIDENCE OF SPIRITUAL FRUIT

So how can we know if there is spiritual fruit in our lives? Jesus gives us four reassuring indications.

1. You will pray with power and results: "If you abide in Me, and My words abide in you, you will ask what you desire, and it shall be done for you." What a promise! However, prayer is not a way of getting God to do what we want. That is why the whole concept of the so-called faith movement, which could be more appropriately called the presumption movement, is so absurd. It alleges that faith is a force that must be harnessed and used, that we must believe and confess what we want, and that we can undo what we pray for by doubting.

I don't know about you, but I don't always know what is good for me spiritually. So to the best of my ability, I will pray for certain things, but at the same time, I'll say, "Lord, I may not have all the information here, so not my will, but Yours, be done." Those in the faith movement would warn against praying something like that. "It's a negative confession," they would say. If that is the case, then Jesus had a negative confession when He prayed in Gethsemane, "Nevertheless not My will, but Yours, be done" (Luke 22:42). He prayed this not once, but three times.

Prayer is not a way of getting God to do what we want, but a process of joining in partnership with God so He can achieve His promises through us. Nothing lies outside the reach of prayer except that which lies outside the will of God. "Now this is the confidence that we have in Him, that if we ask anything according to His will, He hears us. And if we know that He hears us, whatever we ask, we know that we have the petitions that we have asked of Him" (1 John 5:14). Prayer is surrender—surrender to the will of God and cooperation with that will. It's like being on a boat, throwing the boat hook to the shore, and pulling. Do I pull the shore to me? Or do I pull myself to the shore? Prayer is not pulling God to my will, but aligning my will with the will of God.

A life that is not bearing spiritual fruit actually can turn people away from Christ.

Having said all that, when God's Word's is at home in us, we will find ourselves praying according to His will and seeing Him answer in the affirmative. And we will find the Holy Spirit prompting us to pray for certain things. So think about it for a moment: Have you grown deeper in your prayer life? Have you been seeing more of your prayers answered in the affirmative? If so, then you are bearing fruit for Christ.

2. *Your life will glorify* God. Jesus said, "By this My Father is glorified, that you bear much fruit; so you will be My disciples" (v. 8). The greatest advertisement for Jesus Christ is a changed life. Maybe you've personally seen how God has used a life dedicated to Christ to touch people. A classic example of this was the man who was born blind and then was healed by Jesus. There was the evidence of change, along with his testimony: "One thing I know: that though I was blind, now I see" (John 9:25). People may remember you for

who you were before you made a commitment to Christ. Can they see a tangible difference in you between then and now? As it's been said, "If you were arrested for being a Christian, would there be enough evidence to prove you were guilty?"

———

The fruit of the Spirit grows only in the garden of obedience.

———

A life that is not bearing spiritual fruit actually can turn people away from Christ. I am always encouraging believers to tell others about Jesus Christ, with one exception. Not every person who claims to be a follower of Jesus should tell others, because for some who really don't want to follow Christ and obey Him, they do more harm than good. If you are going to drive over the speed limit, and carelessly as well, then don't put Christian symbols or bumper stickers on your car. If you are not going to honor your marriage vows or tell the truth or live with integrity, then please do other Christians a favor and keep your "faith" to yourself. In reality, it is not really faith at all, but a mere façade. The Bible says, "Faith by itself, if it does not have works, is dead" (James 4:17).

So if people have noticed the change in your lifestyle, attitudes, and behavior, if they have asked what has happened to you, then you are being fruitful.

3. You will lovingly obey God's commandments. "If you keep My commandments, you will abide in My love, just as I have kept My Father's commandments and abide in His love" (v. 10). There are so many today who claim to be Christians, but they do not obey Jesus. Yet the fruit of the Spirit grows only in the garden of obedience. If you are truly abiding in Him, then obeying His commandments will not be a burden to you. The apostle John wrote, "If someone says, 'I belong to God,' but doesn't obey God's commandments, that person is a liar and does not live in the truth. But those who obey God's word really do love him. That is the way to know whether or not we live in him" (1 John 2:3–5 NLT). Knowing and loving God is not merely professing Christ, attending church, or even reading the Bible and praying. It is doing what He tells us to do—not perfectly, of course. We will sin, and we will fail. But if we are true children of God, then we will repent and return to Him. Again John wrote, "They went out from us, but they were not of us; for if they had been of us, they would have continued with us; but they went out that they might be made manifest, that none of them were of us" (1 John 2:19).

―――⊰⊱―――

The joy of a Christian runs deeper than mere happiness.

―――⊰⊱―――

It may seem like keeping God's commandments is too difficult and unrealistic in the world we live in. But Jesus said, "My yoke is easy and My burden is light" (Matt. 11:30). And 1 John 5:2–3 tells us, "Now by this we know that we love the children of God, when we love God and keep His commandments. For this is the love of God, that we keep His commandments. And His commandments are not burdensome."

The person who really knows God comes to understand that when God tells us to do or not do something, it is for our own good. It would be like a child complaining to his parent, "Why won't you let me play on the freeway? Caleb's mom lets him play on the freeway!"

4. Your life will have overflowing joy. "These things I have spoken to you," Jesus said, "that My joy may remain in you, and that your joy may be full" (v. 11). The joy of a Christian runs deeper than mere happiness. It does not depend on circumstances; it only depends on God.

Notice the progression of Jesus' words in verse 11 from "My joy" to "your joy." Do you have joy in your life right now? You often can tell someone is a Christian by his or her countenance. Awhile back, I ran into someone who had gone to our church for years, but whom I hadn't seen in some time. You could just tell something was different. The joy was gone. This doesn't mean Christians should walk around with phony smiles plastered across their faces. But even as a person who is abiding in Christ has a life marked with joy, a person who is not abiding in Christ lacks it.

Not only does God want your joy to be continual, but He also wants it to overflow.

Notice Jesus said, "That My joy may *remain* in you" (emphasis mine). When we sin, we lose that joy, and that is why David, after sinning, wrote, "Restore to me the joy of Your salvation, and uphold me by Your generous Spirit" (Ps. 51:12).

It is not that David's salvation was lost, but his joy had evaporated. Not only does God want your joy to be continual, but He also wants it to overflow, that your joy might be full.

Answered prayer, a life glorifying the God who made us, a life of obedience, a life of joy, a life of purpose … these are all evidence of a fruitful Christian life.

May God help us to bear fruit for Him and to fulfill our purpose in life.

4 | THE
HOLY SPIRIT

John 16:7–11

A Sunday School teacher was speaking on the subject of sin and asked the class if they knew the difference between the sins of commission and omission. A little girl in the front of the class raised her hand, so the teacher called on her and asked, "Do you know the definition of the sin of commission?"

"Yes, I do," the girl said. "The sin of commission is when we do what we are not supposed to do."

"That is exactly right," the teacher said. "Now, does anyone know what the sin of omission is?"

A little boy in the back of the room was frantically waving his hand, so the teacher called on him.

He stood up and said, "The sin of omission? Well, those are the sins you want to do, but you just haven't gotten around to them yet."

Not quite. But it does bring up an interesting subject about sin in general. Are some sins worse

than others? And if so, what is the worst sin a
person can commit? You might be surprised
by the answer.

In John 16, we will look at the work of the Holy
Spirit in our lives. And through Jesus' own words,
we will see what He came to do:

> Nevertheless I tell you the truth. It is to your
> advantage that I go away; for if I do not go
> away, the Helper will not come to you; but if
> I depart, I will send Him to you. And when
> He has come, He will convict the world of
> sin, and of righteousness, and of judgment:
> of sin, because they do not believe in Me; of
> righteousness, because I go to My Father and
> you see Me no more; of judgment, because
> the ruler of this world is judged. (vv. 7–11)

NOT "IT"

The Holy Spirit is not an "it" or a force, but a
definite personality. Through Scripture, we clearly
see that the Holy Spirit has a will, emotion, and
intelligence. None of these things are true of an
object or a force. The Holy Spirit has come to
indwell and empower the Christian. As part of
that great work of conversion, He seals us:

> In Him you also trusted, after you heard the

word of truth, the gospel of your salvation;
in whom also, having believed, you were
sealed with the Holy Spirit of promise, who
is the guarantee of our inheritance until the
redemption of the purchased possession, to
the praise of His glory. (Eph. 1:13–14)

---

*The Holy Spirit is not an "it" or
a force, but a definite personality.*

The Holy Spirit also can be called "the deposit
guaranteeing our inheritance." It's like putting
down cash to hold something—a deposit. God
wants you to know that He is sincere about
redeeming you. He intends to complete His
transaction. He won't back down or change
His mind. So, He gives us the deposit, or down
payment, of the Holy Spirit in our lives to show
us that He means business.

OUR HELPER AND TEACHER

Not only does the Spirit bring about the work of
conversion, but as a result, He seals us, teaches us,
and leads us to truth. Jesus said, "But the Helper,
the Holy Spirit, whom the Father will send in My

name, He will teach you all things, and bring to your remembrance all things that I said to you" (John 14:26). The Holy Spirit can, in an incredible way, open up passages of Scripture for us. It comes through our reading and study of God's Word. Needless to say, this is why we need to regularly spend time in Bible study, so we are opening the door for the Holy Spirit to illuminate God's Word to us. There are certain passages that can be difficult to grasp, but the good news is that the same Holy Spirit who inspired the Scripture can also illuminate it for our benefit:

> "Eye has not seen, nor ear heard, nor have entered into the heart of man the things which God has prepared for those who love Him." But God has revealed them to us through His Spirit. For the Spirit searches all things, yes, the deep things of God. For what man knows the things of a man except the spirit of the man which is in him? Even so no one knows the things of God except the Spirit of God. (1 Cor. 2:9–11)

Some people today are looking for "new revelations," but the Holy Spirit is not looking to bring new revelations outside the realm of the Bible. We don't need a different revelation from what God has given us in His Word.

But the Holy Spirit makes these truths alive in our hearts in a personal way.

There is no conversion without conviction.

Sometimes when we are at a church service or Bible study listening to a message being given, a certain point or series of truths really hit home. We are tempted to think, "That person is the greatest preacher of all time." But it's really the Holy Spirit teaching you, because the very truths that impacted you may not necessarily be the same ones the Holy Spirit impressed on someone else.

Then there are times when you are ministering to a fellow believer or sharing the gospel with someone when suddenly verses start coming to mind that you didn't realize you even knew. It was quite possibly the Holy Spirit bringing them to mind for that very moment.

AT WORK IN THE WORLD

So we see there are so many things the Holy Spirit does for us: He is with us. He empowers us. He seals us. And He teaches us. But what is the work the Holy Spirit wants to do in the world, or in the life of the unbeliever? We find the answer in verse 8: "And when He has come, He will convict the world of sin, and of righteousness, and of judgment. ..." You see, one's ignorance of sin, righteousness, and judgment can ultimately bring about their destruction. So God has sent the Holy Spirit to make the unbeliever aware of this. People need to be convicted by the Holy Spirit, because there is no conversion without conviction.

The Holy Spirit shows the unbeliever his or her need for God.

Otherwise, why convert? Is it to simply have a better life? By the way some people present the gospel, you would think that is all there is. You would think that Christianity is a type of self-help program. It's as though they are saying, "You know, if you want a little more spring in your step, or a better marriage, or if you want to be a happy person, then believe in Jesus, and it will happen."

Don't get me wrong: I'm not dismissing the fact that Jesus can make a marriage better. Nor am I suggesting that He will not make you happy, because indeed He will. But what I am saying is the work God has come to do for you is so much more than these things. They are the fringe benefits. The ultimate work that God has come to do for you is to save you from your sin and its ramifications—in essence, judgment. So the Holy Spirit makes you aware of the fact that you are a sinner desperately in need of salvation. He brings about the work of conviction in your heart. The word used in verse 8 for "convict" means "to cross-examine with the purpose of convicting or refuting an opponent." He does not simply convict the world in general, but specifically shows unbelievers they are lacking in righteousness, they have sinned, and as a result, they will face a future judgment.

The Bible uses the words "trespass" and "sin." To trespass is to deliberately cross a line, but sin carries an additional meaning: "to miss the mark." This is not speaking so much of "sins," but of "sin"—to miss the mark.

The Holy Spirit shows the unbeliever his or her need for God. And as much we may want to produce in someone a sense of guilt and wrongdoing, only the Holy Spirit can effectively do so. In fact, we can even hinder the process of

conversion when we interfere in the work of the
Holy Spirit. Well-meaning but misguided believers
can resort to pressure tactics. But if someone
can be pressured into conversion, they also can
be pressured out. We need to proclaim the truth
and then pray for the Holy Spirit to do His work
of conviction. On the day of Pentecost, Peter
preached the gospel, and the Holy Spirit was at
work. The Bible tells us that the people who were
listening were "cut to the heart" (Acts 2:37). The
word "cut" used in this verse means "to pierce," or
"to stab," thus indicating something sudden and
unexpected occurred, something that only the
Holy Spirit could bring about. The people then
asked Peter, "What shall we do?" So Peter led
them all to Christ.

THE "WORST" SIN

This brings us back to our earlier question: What
is the worst sin that you can commit? Is it murder,
adultery, or stealing? Is it taking the Lord's name
in vain? Is it rape or incest? While these are all
terrible sins, the "worst" sin—and the one with
the most far-reaching consequences—is not
believing in Jesus Christ. It may be difficult to

understand how any sin could be worse than sins such as murder and adultery. But these are simply outgrowths of the sin inside a person who does not know God or is clearly in rebellion against Him, which is the root of all our problems. The worst possible sin we can commit is not believing, because that is what we will be judged for. All sins can be dealt with and forgiven if we believe in Him.

We can even hinder the process of conversion when we interfere in the work of the Holy Spirit.

In addition to showing the unbeliever his or her need for God, the Holy Spirit has come to bring us to Jesus: "And when He has come, He will convict the world of sin … because they do not believe in Me" (vv. 8–9). Once we've heard the gospel, that knowledge brings responsibility. Jesus said, "If I had not come and spoken to them, they would have no sin, but now they have no excuse for their sin" (John 15:22).

By our refusal to believe in Jesus Christ as the Son of God, who bore the sins of the world, we are rejecting the very work of the Holy Spirit (see vv. 13–14). If we refuse to believe, we are essentially calling the Holy Spirit a liar, because we are rejecting the record God gave of His Son: "He who believes in the Son of God has the witness in himself; he who does not believe God has made Him a liar, because he has not believed the testimony that God has given of His Son" (1 John 5:10).

OUR NEED FOR CONVICTION

The Holy Spirit also has come to show us our need for righteousness. Jesus said that when the Holy Spirit has come, "He will convict the world of sin, and of righteousness, … because I go to My Father and you see Me no more" (vv. 8, 10). The apostle Paul tells us "the unrighteous will not inherit the kingdom of God" (1 Cor. 6:9). And Jesus said that unless our righteousness exceeds that of the scribes and Pharisees, we cannot enter the kingdom of heaven (see Matt. 5:20). I remember reading this as a young believer and thinking, "How could my righteousness possibly surpass theirs?" I knew the scribes and Pharisees were devoutly religious men. But then I realized this was not a righteousness that I could personally produce. In fact, even on my best day, my righteousness is pretty much worthless, because the Bible says, "All our righteousnesses are like filthy rags…" (Isa. 64:6). So for the proud, self-confident individual who thinks he doesn't need Jesus because of the exemplary life he lives (or thinks he does), the Holy Spirit comes with His convicting, convincing power and sets him straight.

If someone can be pressured into conversion, they also can be pressured out.

When we believe in Jesus and are justified as a result, His righteousness is deposited into our spiritual account. So before people can totally appreciate the incredible love of God, they must first see their utter depravity and desperate need for a Savior. But this is very hard for most people. We like to think that we have something to do with it. We're like the man who was out hiking in the mountains, lost his footing, and slipped over the side—a one-hundred-foot drop. Fortunately, he grabbed hold of a branch on the way down and hung on to it for dear life. Knowing he was in real trouble, he cried out for help. But there was no answer. Again he cried out. Again it was quiet.

The third time he yelled, "Is there anybody out there?"

A voice responded, "Yes, I am here."

"Who are you?" the man called back.

"I am the Lord," the voice said.

"Well, Lord, help me!"

"I will. But I need you to do something first."

"What?" he yelled back.

"Let go of the branch."

"That's crazy!" the man shouted. "If I let go of the branch, I will fall to my death."

"No," the Lord said, "I will catch you."

There was a moment of silence, then the man yelled out, "Is anybody else up there?"

Like that hiker, we are clinging firmly to our branch of self-righteousness. We don't want to let go. We think, "I am a moral person. I am a good person. I am a religious person."

But God says, "No, you have to realize that you need to be forgiven. You need to come and admit you are a sinner." This is hard for a lot of people to do. But we must let go of the flimsy branch of self-righteousness that actually keeps us from the true righteousness of God. True righteousness is not available to us until we have an awareness of sin, and the Holy Spirit has come to help us discover this.

KEEPING THE LID ON

Furthermore, the Holy Spirit, working through the church, acts as a restraining force in the world today. In speaking of the Holy Spirit, the Bible says, "For the mystery of lawlessness is already at work; only He who now restrains will do so until He is taken out of the way" (2 Thess. 2:7). Or as another translation puts it, "For the secret power of lawlessness is already at work; but the one who now holds it back will continue to do so till he is taken out of the way" (NIV).

As we look at our world today and see the wanton, senseless violence and the disregard for human life, it really is frightening. And I have some bad news: it will get worse. As we read about life in this world in the Book of Revelation, we know the worst days are still ahead, with the emergence of the Antichrist and demonic powers running amok.

But I also have some good news: Jesus Christ will come back for His church and remove us from

the Earth before the worst happens. Presently, the
Holy Spirit is the One who is at work, restraining
the complete outbreak of "the mystery of
lawlessness" that 2 Thessalonians speaks of. He is
the One holding the lid on this world's boiling keg
of violence. But once the Holy Spirit removes
the church and no longer restrains evil, the
powers of darkness will take over.

PRESERVING AND SHINING

One of the ways the Holy Spirit restrains evil
is through believers. Jesus has told us, as His
children, to act as both salt and light in this
world (see Matt. 5:13–16).

*True righteousness is not available to us
until we have an awareness of sin.*

Salt functioned as a preservative in ancient
times, and in the same way, God uses us to
stand up for what is right and true and to try
to stop the wholesale spread of evil in our
culture. This means living as true, Bible-
believing Christians to the extent that our

faith influences everything we do and say, such as the friends we choose, the media we expose ourselves to, and the decision we make. Tragically, far too many today are being squeezed into the world's mold. Jesus warned, "If the salt loses its flavor, how shall it be seasoned? It is then good for nothing but to be thrown out and trampled underfoot by men" (Matt. 5:13).

To be light means that we are to let others know of our faith in Christ. Jesus said, "Let your light so shine before men, that they may see your good works and glorify your Father in heaven" (Matt. 5:16). But we also read in John 1:5, "The light shines in the darkness, and the darkness did not comprehend it." In its original language, the word "comprehend" carries the meaning of "understood." Often in our attempt to avoid being perceived as fanatical by unbelievers, we try to relate to them. But they can plainly see there is something different about us—something major. The apostle Paul recognized this when he wrote to the Corinthians, "Don't team up with those who are unbelievers. How can goodness be a partner with wickedness? How can light live with darkness? What harmony can there be between

Christ and the Devil? How can a believer be a partner with an unbeliever? (2 Cor. 6:14–15 NLT). Try as you may to relate as hard as you can, unbelievers simply will not understand your faith and commitment to Christ until their spiritual eyes are opened, because the Bible tells us, "The natural man does not receive the things of the Spirit of God, for they are foolishness to him; nor can he know them, because they are spiritually discerned" (1 Cor. 2:14).

Tragically, far too many today are being squeezed into the world's mold.

I know this is frustrating for many believers who, more than anything else, want their friends and family to come to know this Jesus who has done so much for them. Consider the fact that when you're sound asleep in the early hours of the morning, when it is still dark outside, you are not usually pleased when someone flips on the light and tells you to wake up. In the same way, realize that it is the very process of being uncomfortable around true Christians that ultimately will help to spiritually awaken an unbeliever. Before unbelievers can see their desperate need for the light, they must first see they are living in a miserable darkness. Before there can be conversion, there must be conviction—and that will come through believers as the Holy Spirit works through them, as they live godly lives, and as they share the gospel. Believers are making a mistake if they try and undo the very thing God is using in the lives of unbelievers to show them their need for Him. Unbelievers have a choice in the matter, and if they refuse to listen, they might insult the Holy Spirit.

INSULTING THE SPIRIT

How would we actually insult the Holy Spirit? The ultimate insult would be to reject what He wants to show us, which is our need for Jesus Christ. Let's say, for example, that it was your birthday, and I went to great expense to buy you a present. I spent everything I had for this gift, but you wouldn't even look at it. "That's so sweet of you," you say, "but really, you shouldn't have. I don't really want it. Maybe some other time. Bye-bye."

By saying no to the Holy Spirit time and time again, we will find ourselves resisting Him.

And if we continue on this path, it could ultimately lead to blaspheming the Holy Spirit, the only unforgivable sin.

A LESSON FROM THE EARLY CHURCH

To understand this further, let's go to the Book of Acts, where we are introduced to sins that can be committed against the Holy Spirit. As I mentioned earlier, the Holy Spirit is not just a force; He is a personality. And the Bible identifies things we do that can offend Him.

Now the early church was so close to God and so pure, that one, significant event took place that stunned a lot of people. It was a sin committed by Ananias and his wife Sapphira, who thought they could fool God and pretend to be something they were not. From their story, we discover some specific sins that can be committed against the Holy Spirit:

> But a certain man named Ananias, with
> Sapphira his wife, sold a possession. And he
> kept back part of the proceeds, his wife also
> being aware of it, and brought a certain part
> and laid it at the apostles' feet. But Peter
> said, "Ananias, why has Satan filled your
> heart to lie to the Holy Spirit and keep

back part of the price of the land for yourself? While it remained, was it not your own? And after it was sold, was it not in your own control? Why have you conceived this thing in your heart? You have not lied to men but to God." Then Ananias, hearing these words, fell down and breathed his last. So great fear came upon all those who heard these things. (Acts 5:1–5)

Some important truths about the Holy Spirit stand out in this text. One is that the Holy Spirit is God. Peter asked Ananias, "Why has Satan filled your heart *to lie to the Holy Spirit*?" (v. 3, emphasis mine), and told him, "You have not lied to men but to God" (v. 4). This reminds us that the Holy Spirit is One who can be specifically lied to. What was this sin of lying to the Holy Spirit all about? The sin of Ananias and Sapphira was pretending to be something they were not. They were hypocrites. Ananias wanted people to think that he was thoroughly devoted to God, when, in fact, he wasn't. As Cicero said, "Of all villainy, there is none more base than that of the hypocrite, who, at the moment he is most false, takes care to appear most virtuous."

This sin has been repeated many times throughout church history and continues to this day. In speaking of the wayward children of Israel, God said, "These people draw near with their mouths and honor Me with their lips, but have removed their hearts far from Me …" (Isa. 29:13). This was the same sin that Judas Iscariot committed, among others, as he kissed the Lord repeatedly. Today, this sin continues when people come to church and go through the motions, but don't really mean it in their heart of hearts. We should be thankful that God doesn't deal with us today in the same way He dealt with Ananias and Sapphira.

SIX SINS AGAINST THE HOLY SPIRIT

The New Testament mentions six offenses that can be committed against the Holy Spirit. Some specifically apply to unbelievers, while others apply to believers, though there may be some that apply to both.

One, we can lie to the Holy Spirit, as we've already seen from the example of Ananias and Sapphira.

Two, we can grieve the Holy Spirit. This offense applies to believers. Ephesians 4:30–31 tells us, "And do not grieve the Holy Spirit of God, by whom you were sealed for the day of redemption. Let all bitterness, wrath, anger, clamor, and evil speaking be put away from you, with all malice." The phrase "to grieve" means "to make sad or sorrowful." When we allow bitterness, rage, anger, harsh words, slander, and any type of malicious behavior to take place in our lives, we grieve the Holy Spirit. Are you harboring a grudge against someone? Have you been slandering (speaking lies about) anyone lately? Have you been flying into fits of rage? All of this grieves the Holy Spirit.

The sin of Ananias and Sapphira was pretending to be something they were not.

Three, we can quench the Holy Spirit. This, too, applies to believers. The apostle Paul exhorted the Thessalonians, "Do not quench the Spirit" (1 Thess. 5:19). The thought of "quenching" suggests extinguishing a fire, and unbelief certainly can hinder the working and moving of God's Holy Spirit. This happened in Jesus' hometown as the people questioned His authority. We read that "He did not do many mighty works there because of their unbelief" (Matt. 13:58). Quenching the Spirit can occur when the Holy Spirit is leading you to do a certain thing, such as sharing your faith with someone, praying more, or taking a step of faith in a certain area, and you flatly refuse to do that. Has God called you to serve Him with your life? Has He led you to do something? Are you doing it? If not, then you're quenching the Holy Spirit.

⸻◦◈◦⸻

Unbelief certainly can hinder the working and moving of God's Holy Spirit.

⸻◦◈◦⸻

Four, we can resist the Holy Spirit. Stephen, as he spoke to the unbelieving Sanhedrin, said, "You stubborn people! You are heathen at heart and deaf to the truth. Must you forever resist the Holy Spirit? But your ancestors did, and so do you!" (Acts 7:51 NLT). The Holy Spirit seeks to speak to the heart of the unbeliever and lead him or her to God. The Holy Spirit is incredibly patient and persistent, but it is possible to resist all His pleadings, as we discover from Genesis 6:3, where God said, "My Spirit shall not strive with man forever…." Apparently the spiritual leaders of Israel whom Stephen was addressing had resisted the Holy Spirit. It seems they were convinced of the truth of what Stephen was telling them, yet they would not yield their hearts.

Fifth, we can insult the Holy Spirit. This is a sin that unbelievers can commit. It is the office of the Holy Spirit to present the saving work of Jesus Christ to the unbeliever. But when someone refuses to accept Jesus Christ, he is really denying the very mission of the Holy Spirit and is saying that he doesn't need salvation or doesn't believe Jesus Christ can save him or that Jesus' work on the cross was unnecessary. Hebrews warns, "Of how much worse punishment, do you suppose, will he be thought worthy who has trampled the Son of God underfoot, counted the blood of the covenant by which he was sanctified a common thing, and insulted the Spirit of grace?" (Heb. 10:29). Therefore, to resist the Holy Spirit's appeal is to insult God and cut off all hope of salvation. The Bible poses this alarming question: "How shall we escape if we neglect so great a salvation?…" (Heb. 2:3).

Sixth, we can blaspheme the Holy Spirit. This is the unpardonable sin, which can be committed only by unbelievers. In speaking of this sin, Jesus said,

> "Therefore I say to you, every sin and blasphemy will be forgiven men, but the blasphemy against the Spirit will not be forgiven men. Anyone who speaks a word against the Son of Man, it will be forgiven him; but whoever speaks against the Holy Spirit, it will not be forgiven him, either in this age or in the age to come."
> (Matt. 12:31–32)

This is the most serious offense against the Holy Spirit, because there is no forgiveness for the one who commits it. So what is blasphemy against the Holy Spirit? Again, the work of the Holy Spirit is to convict us of sin and bring us to Jesus Christ. To blaspheme Him is similar to insulting Him, in that we resist His work altogether. It no doubt follows the pattern of resisting Him, insulting Him, and ultimately leading to this horrendous sin.

This sin should not be the concern of any Christian, because it is not a sin a believer can or will commit.

But for the person who is playing some silly religious game, there is great cause for concern, because this is a point of no return. Where and when this would occur in an individual's life, only God could say.

This is the most serious offense against the Holy Spirit, because there is no forgiveness for the one who commits it.

So instead of lying to, grieving, quenching, or insulting and resisting the Holy Spirit, we should be open to His work in our lives. He wants to show us our need for Jesus Christ and then fill and empower us to be the people God wants us to be.

JESUS' PRAYER FOR YOU

John 17

Sometimes people will ask me to pray for them or to remember them in prayer. And I'll admit that it's something I haven't always done as well as I should. I will try and pray with them right then, because later, I may forget their names. (Thankfully, God doesn't.)

We want others to pray for us, and so we should, because clearly there is power in united prayer. Jesus said, "Again I say to you that if two of you agree on earth concerning anything that they ask, it will be done for them by My Father in heaven" (Matt. 18:19).

I appreciate it when people pray for me, especially when our large-scale evangelistic outreaches we call Harvest Crusades are underway. It is during these times that the spiritual battle rages, and it seems as though I can actually feel the prayers being said for me, if that is possible. I am buoyed by a power that is supernatural.

We all should remember to pray for one another, but even if we do forget, there is some good news: Jesus Christ himself is praying for you. Hebrews tells us, "Therefore He is also able to save to the uttermost those who come to God through Him, since He always lives to make intercession for them" (Heb. 7:25). And we read in Romans 8:34, "Who is he who condemns? It is Christ who died, and furthermore is also risen, who is even at the right hand of God, who also makes intercession for us."

THE GREATEST PRAYER EVER PRAYED

So when Jesus intercedes for us, what does He pray about? This is important for us to know, because in the discovery of it, we will know His plan and purpose for our lives. And isn't that the objective of prayer, after all—to align our will with God's will?

In John 17, we find the answer to that question as we see Jesus' prayer for His disciples—past, present, and future. It is Jesus' prayer for you. And it is the greatest prayer ever prayed.

We call the prayer that Jesus gave to His disciples "The Lord's Prayer," but in reality, it is "The Disciples' Prayer." This prayer contains petitions that Jesus would never need to make, such as "Forgive us our debts, as we forgive our debtors...."

Jesus Christ himself is praying for you.

In John 17 we find the true "Lord's Prayer." This prayer contains petitions that only Jesus could ask. It shows God's heart, His desire, and His purpose for you.

The first thing worth noting is that Jesus prayed to begin with. Why would Jesus, a member of the Trinity, need to pray? Yet throughout the Gospels, we see that He prayed regularly. After a dizzying, busy day of ministry, He would spend the entire evening coming before His Father. Often He would spend all night in prayer. And before He selected the twelve disciples, we are told that He prayed all night (see Luke 6:12–13). He was praying when He was transfigured with Moses and Elijah. Later, we see Him praying in anguish in the Garden of Gethsemane. The first words that fell from His lips when He hung from the cross formed a prayer. And later on the cross, He also prayed, "My God, My God, why have You forsaken Me?" (Mark 15:34).

Without a doubt, Jesus was a man of prayer.

But why? Because although He was God, Jesus submitted to the Father. Not only that, but He was leaving us an example to follow. If Jesus, who was perfect and sinless, took time to pray, then how much more should we, as imperfect and sinful people, do the same?

Without a doubt,
Jesus was a man of prayer.

It is also worth noting that Jesus prayed out loud, where His disciples could hear. His prayer wasn't directed to them, but He wanted them to hear it. He wanted them to see the special place they held in His holy heart.

His prayer in John 17 can be divided into three sections:

1. Jesus first prayed for himself (vv. 1–5). He told the Father that His work on Earth was finished.

2. Jesus prayed for His disciples (vv. 6–19). He prayed that the Father would keep and sanctify them.

3. Jesus closed the prayer by praying for

you, me, and the entire church to come
(vv. 20–26).

A PRAYER FOR HIMSELF

Jesus started by praying for himself, which, by
the way, is not a bad thing to do. As R. A. Torrey
once said, "A prayer for self is not by any means
necessarily a selfish prayer." So Jesus began,
"Father, the hour has come …" (v. 1). Jesus had
used this phrase again and again throughout His
earthly ministry. When His mother wanted Him
to show His power at the wedding in Cana, He
responded, "Woman, what does your concern have
to do with Me? My hour has not yet come" (John
2:4). Then in John 7, we read that the religious
leaders were angry with Jesus and wanted to arrest
him: "Therefore they sought to take Him; but no
one laid a hand on Him, because His hour had not
yet come" (John 7:30).

But now, the hour has come, the hour of His
betrayal, arrest, crucifixion, and resurrection from
the dead. It was the hour of both darkness and
light, the hour of Satan's attack, and the hour of
our purchased salvation. Jesus had finished the
work the Father had given Him to do. Earlier in

this Gospel, Jesus said, "The Father has not left Me alone, for I always do those things that please Him" (John 8:29). And that was 100-percent true. He had glorified the Father in all He said and did, from the beginning to the end of His earthly ministry. And certainly He left us an example to follow. The Bible tells us, "Let this mind be in you which was also in Christ Jesus…" (Phil 2:5). I am here on this earth to glorify and know the God who created me. And so are you. We read in 1 Peter 2:9, "But you are a chosen generation, a royal priesthood, a holy nation, His own special people, that you may proclaim the praises of Him who called you out of darkness into His marvelous light."

Sometimes we forget this. We think that we are here to be happy. But the Bible does not teach that our purpose is to be happy. Rather, we are here to know and glorify the God who made us. And we are to be holy. Then happiness becomes the by-product of a holy life. So if your life is going reasonably well right now, if your job is doing well, if you are having a successful ministry, or if you are in good health, then praise God. Give Him the glory for it. Carry out your ministry, do your job, and live your life to bring praise to the Lord.

However, another thing to keep in mind is that God also can be glorified through our suffering. In John 9, we find the story of a man who was born blind, whom Jesus healed. The disciples asked an age-old question: "Why was this man born blind?" Or, as it is more often stated, "Why does God allow suffering?"

We are here to know and glorify the God who made us.

Jesus told them, "Neither this man nor his parents sinned, but that the works of God should be revealed in him. I must work with works of Him who sent Me while it is day; the night is coming when no one can work" (John 9:3–4). God can be glorified as a believer honors Him, despite the suffering. Jesus didn't really deal with the issue or the question they asked, but He was essentially saying, "God is going to be glorified through this." I cannot always explain why there is suffering. We know ultimately that it is a result of the curse of humanity called sin. I don't know that we can answer a lot of the questions this side of heaven about why God allows suffering or certain calamities. But I do know this much: God can be glorified through our suffering. It is a powerful testimony to a lost world.

God can be glorified through our suffering. It is a powerful testimony to a lost world.

I think of someone like Dave Dravecky, a great athlete and former Major League Baseball pitcher who shared his testimony at a Harvest Crusade a number of years ago. Dave was diagnosed with cancer, which claimed his right arm and shoulder. Obviously, it was a devastating setback, yet Dave has now committed his life to ministering to people. I had the opportunity to talk at length with him about how he was feeling and asked him if he had any pain. He said he had phantom pain where his arm used to be and is in pain throughout the day. That is typical, he said. But God gives him the strength to endure it. He visits cancer wards in hospitals, speaks in churches, and glorifies God, in spite of his infirmity.

Then there is Lt. Col. Brian Birdwell, who was working at the Pentagon on September 11, 2001 when American Flight 77 was commandeered by terrorists and crashed into the Pentagon building. Birdwell was severely burned, and a number of his coworkers were killed. He went through very painful skin grafts, enduring more than thirty operations. Yet now he travels around ministering and glorifying God, despite his infirmity.

The apostle Paul, in writing about his own "thorn in the flesh," said, "So now I am glad to boast about my weaknesses, so that the power of Christ may work through me. Since I know it is all for Christ's good, I am quite content with my weaknesses and with insults, hardships, persecutions, and calamities. For when I am weak, then I am strong" (2 Cor. 12:9–10 NIV).

So there are times when God is glorified in the midst of our infirmities, and there are times in which He is glorified by the removal of them. That was the case with the blind man from John 9. But our objective should be to glorify God, regardless of the temporary outcome. Again, we can look to the apostle Paul as an example. He wrote, "I know what it is to be in need, and I know what it is to have plenty. I have learned the secret of being content in any and every situation, whether well fed or hungry, whether living in plenty or in want. I can do everything through him who gives me strength" (Phil. 4:12–13 NIV).

———◆———

If there is a sin we are all probably guilty of, it is the sin of prayerlessness.

———◆———

Let me be clear: I don't want to come across as cavalier about personal tragedies, because if you are the one who is suffering, it is no easy task. But God will give you the power you need to face that challenge or obstacle. Many of us wonder why God allows certain things in our lives, but what we fail to see is what God is doing *internally* to change us. These verses help put things into perspective:

> For our present troubles are quite small and won't last very long. Yet they produce for us an immeasurably great glory that will last forever! So we don't look at the troubles we can see right now; rather, we look forward to what we have not yet seen. For the troubles we see will soon be over, but the joys to come will last forever. (2 Cor. 4:17–18 NLT)

This brings us back to the "why" of prayer. I believe God allows certain circumstances in our lives to keep us dependent on Him. If life were all blue skies and green lights, would we turn to God in prayer? If there were never an illness in your life or the life of someone you knew, would you still pray? If there were never a need for provision or never a prodigal child, would you still pray? You might, but probably not as often or as fervently.

In his book, *When God Prays*, my friend Skip Heitzig tells the story of a father whose son was leaving for college. This father came up with an effective way to maintain contact with his son. He had agreed to pay his son's tuition and also give him a monthly allowance for the next four years so he could fully concentrate on his studies. But before the boy left home, his father sat him down for a talk.

He was praying that our faith would not fail.

"Now Son, your Mom and I are really glad that you're going to school," he told him. "And just as I promised, I'll be taking care of your financial needs for the next four years.... But I won't be sending you a monthly check."

The boy was puzzled. "What? But you said—"

"What I said was that I would be providing for your needs on a monthly basis," his father answered. "If you want the money, you'll have to come home at least once a month to get it. I want you to come in person."

This wise father knew that his son might get caught up in his new environment and not want to come home very often. So to preserve a relationship with his son and enjoy his occasional fellowship, he made sure the boy would come around often enough to touch base.[1]

God allows challenges in our lives so we will not forget Him and will come to Him in prayer. If there is a sin we are all probably guilty of, it is the sin of prayerlessness. Often we have forgotten God when things are going well, and we sometimes forget that our purpose on this earth is glorifying Him. A. W. Tozer offered this helpful test for determining whether we are glorifying God with our lives: What is it that we want the most? What do we think about the most? How do we use our money? What do we do in our leisure time? What company do we enjoy? Who and what do we admire? And, what do we laugh at?[2]

A PRAYER FOR OUR PRESERVATION

Now let's look at how Jesus prays for His disciples. In this prayer, we see God's heart and God's will for us.

God never forgets what He loves.

First, Jesus prayed for our preservation: "Now I am no longer in the world, but these are in the world, and I come to You. Holy Father, keep through Your name those whom You have given Me, that they may be one as We are" (v. 11). In Luke's Gospel, Jesus turned to Simon Peter at one point and said, "Simon, Simon! Indeed, Satan has asked for you, that he may sift you as wheat. But I have prayed for you, that your faith should not fail; and when you have returned to Me, strengthen your brethren" (Luke 22:31–32). Here in John 17, Jesus was doing the same. He was praying that our faith would not fail.

We all know people who seem to have made a commitment to follow Jesus, only to become a spiritual casualty. Some of them might even have been people whom you looked to as role models. Maybe it has caused you to question, "Am I next? Will I, too, become a spiritual failure?"

The answer to that question is entirely up to you. I would suggest that when people fall away spiritually, it is, for all practical purposes, because they chose to. It is not that they said, "Hey, I think I'll backslide today." Rather, the problem was they no longer were moving forward spiritually. In essence, they put their lives in spiritual cruise control. But if you are not moving forward spiritually, then it is only a matter of time until you fall backward.

Scripture clearly tells us that God will keep us:

I will lift up my eyes to the hills—from whence comes my help? My help comes from the Lord who made heaven and earth. He will not allow your foot to be moved; He who keeps you will not slumber. Behold, He who keeps Israel shall neither slumber nor sleep. The Lord is your keeper; the Lord is your shade at your right hand. The sun shall not strike you by day, nor the moon by night. (Ps. 121:1–5)

*Jesus loves us, preserves us,
and intercedes for us.*

And Scripture also tells us how, time and
again, the Lord instructed the Jewish priests to
pronounce a blessing over the people. He wanted
them to hear it so many times that it would be
etched in the banks of their memories: "The Lord
bless you and keep you; the Lord make His face
shine upon you, and be gracious to you; the Lord
lift up His countenance upon you, and give you
peace" (Num. 6:24–26, emphasis mine).

We find the same truth in the New Testament
as well. In 1 Peter, we see that believers "are *kept
by the power of God* through faith for salvation
ready to be revealed in the last time" (1 Peter
1:5, emphasis mine). And Jude 1 begins, "Jude,
a bondservant of Jesus Christ, and brother of
James, to those who are called, sanctified by
God the Father, and *preserved* in Jesus Christ"
(v. 1, emphasis mine). In the original language,
this verse uses the perfect tense, of which the
nearest equivalent is "continually kept." It is a
continuing result of past action. So whatever

your difficulties may be, know that you are preserved in Jesus Christ.

When you possess something valuable, you are usually aware of where it is. And certainly you don't lose someone you love. You wouldn't go to Disneyland with your kids and then completely forget them and leave. In the same way, God never forgets what He loves. He will protect His investment. A few chapters earlier in John's Gospel, we read that "when Jesus knew that His hour had come that He should depart from this world to the Father, having loved His own who were in the world, He loved them to the end" (John 13:1). If it were not for the preserving grace of God, not a single one of us would make it. But thankfully, Jesus loves us, preserves us, and intercedes for us. So clearly, we are preserved, protected, and kept by the power of God.

Although God will keep us, we must want to be kept.

Although God will keep us, we must *want* to be kept. Which brings up an interesting aspect of Jesus' prayer. He mentioned Judas Iscariot, who had already left to betray Him: "Those whom You gave Me I have kept; and none of them is lost except the son of perdition, that the Scripture might be fulfilled" (v. 12). It wasn't that Judas was a believer who fell away. Judas never was a believer to begin with. Jesus *keeps* all whom the Father has given to Him. Even so, the Bible tells us, "Keep yourselves in the love of God, looking for the mercy of our Lord Jesus Christ unto eternal life (Jude 1:21), showing us that clearly there is God's part, and there is also ours. We don't keep ourselves *saved*, but we do keep ourselves *safe*. Though God's love is unsought, undeserved, and unconditional, it is possible for us to be out of harmony with His love.

So what does Jude mean by telling us to "keep ourselves in the love of God"? Simply put, it means that we are to keep ourselves from all that is unlike God. We are to keep ourselves from any influence that would violate His love and bring sorrow to His heart. It means keeping ourselves in a place where God can actively show and pour out His love in our lives. Some people, places, and activities make it easier for the devil to tempt us. So now that we've been delivered from the kingdom of

Satan, we should have no desire to deliberately put ourselves back into his clutches. When we pray, as Jesus taught, "Lead us not into temptation," we're asking our Heavenly Father to help us so we won't tempt ourselves by deliberately placing ourselves in volatile situations. And this leads us to the next thing Jesus prayed for.

A PRAYER FOR OUR CONSECRATION

Second, Jesus prayed for our consecration:

> "But now I come to You, and these things I speak in *the world*, that they may have My joy fulfilled in themselves. I have given them Your word; and *the world* has hated them because they are not of *the world*, just as I am not of *the world*. I do not pray that You should take them out of *the world*, but that You should keep them from the evil one. They are not of *the world*, just as I am not of *the world*. Sanctify them by Your truth. Your word is truth." (vv. 13–17, emphasis mine)

We are living in an environment which is alien and hostile toward our faith. It's called the world. We need to remember that, because sometimes we get a little too comfortable in this world. As 1 John 2:16 tells us, "For all that is in the world—

the lust of the flesh, the lust of the eyes, and the pride of life—is not of the Father but is of the world." Another translation puts it this way: "For the world offers only the lust for physical pleasure, the lust for everything we see, and pride in our possessions. These are not from the Father. They are from this evil world" (NLT).

It's like scuba diving, a sport that requires special equipment for a special environment. When I became certified a number of years ago, I had to learn about all kinds of equipment. There is your B.C., which is your inflatable vest. Then you have your regulator, your aqua lung that you breathe through, which is hooked up to your tanks. You have gauges that you have to watch. Then you have fins, a mask, a snorkel for when you are not using your regulator, a weight belt, and so forth. As part of my training, I had to go underwater, take off my weight belt, and put it back on again. Then I had to take off my tanks and put them back on. Then there was buddy breathing, so in case I lost air, I could share with another diver. The funny thing is that I was able to cruise through all those things. But the most difficult time came when I had to take off my mask, put it in a little pile, then reach down and find it, put it back on, and clear the water out—all while underwater. There was something about having that mask ripped off my face that suddenly woke me up to the reality that I was underwater. It wasn't that I didn't already know this, but there was a false sense of security behind that glass and that air. Even when I had my oxygen tanks taken away, I wasn't concerned. But when my mask was removed, it was a wake-up call that said, "You are in the ocean, Buddy. And you don't belong down here. This is not your environment."

In the same way, sometimes we get a little bit too comfortable in this world. We start blending in and becoming too much like people around us. So we need our masks removed, so to speak. We need to be reminded that we are not of this world. We sometimes forget this world doesn't love those of us who are followers of Christ. Jesus said of His disciples, "The world has hated them …" (v. 14). Why? Because if we are true followers of Jesus Christ, then our light will shine in a dark world. And those who live in darkness don't welcome bright, searing light. People are not always going to appreciate your stand.

*Sometimes we get a little bit
too comfortable in this world.*

This doesn't mean that we should try and isolate ourselves. Living in a monastery won't actually remove you from the temptations of this life. In fact, no matter where you go, temptation will be there waiting for you. Therefore, we must learn to take hold of God's divine resources to resist temptation. We should seek to influence others as we live our lives for the glory of God. If Jesus had wanted to, He could have immediately transported you to heaven on the day of your conversion. But instead, He has chosen to keep and preserve you in this world. The reason is so that you can reach it with the gospel.

Some Christians, however, seem to live in a "believer's bubble" from sunup to sundown. They talk only with Christians, read only Christian books, listen only to Christian music, watch only Christian TV, and drive a car they purchased from a Christian. While I thank God for the many Christian resources we have available today, I believe Jesus wants us to reach out.

We have a number of choices as to how we will live in this world.

One is *isolation*, in which we have little to no contact with unbelievers. That is a mistake. Then there is *insulation*, where we turn a blind eye to the pain and anguish of those who are without Christ. Next there is *stagnation*. This is living in such a way that we have no impact on the world. We're not growing in the Lord. And worse, there is *imitation*, where we actually are becoming like the world we are supposed to be influencing. We become more like *them* than *Him*. So none of these are the way we should live.

Instead, we should be engaged in *permeation* and *infiltration* as godly people, kept by Christ, wanting to reach out to others. One of the ways we do this is by living a sanctified, or holy, life. Jesus prayed, "Sanctify them by Your truth. Your word is truth" (v. 17). To be "sanctified" means to be "set apart." We read in 2 Timothy 2:20–21, "But in a great house there are not only vessels of gold and silver, but also of wood and clay, some for honor and some for dishonor. Therefore if anyone cleanses himself from the latter, he will be a vessel for honor, *sanctified and useful for the Master,* prepared for every good work" (emphasis mine). A holy and sanctified life is what Jesus wants from us. This is His heart and His desire. When we live holy lives—godly lives—it affects other people. And when we live holy lives, we will live happy lives as well.

A PRAYER FOR OUR UNITY

Third, Jesus prayed that we would be unified:

> "I do not pray for these alone, but also for those who will believe in Me through their word; that they all may be one, as You, Father, are in Me, and I in You; that they also may be one in Us, that the world may believe that You sent Me. And the glory which You gave Me I have given them, that they may be one just as We are one: I in them, and You in Me; that they may be made perfect in one, and that the world may know that You have sent Me, and have loved them as You have loved Me."
> (vv. 20–23)

What a powerful witness to a lost world when Christians are unified and loving one another! Jesus said, "By this all will know that you are My disciples, if you have love for one another"

(John 13:35). And the psalmist wrote, "Behold, how good and how pleasant it for brethren to dwell together in unity!" (Ps. 133:1).

This is why a Harvest Crusade is such a wonderful thing. In addition to carrying out the obvious task of proclaiming the gospel, it brings churches together. There is something wonderful about worshipping and praying with 45,000 people. You realize that you—and those in your local church—aren't the only believers out there.

Yet the devil loves to bring about division. His strategy always has been to divide and conquer. We even see it in the early church: "But as the believers rapidly multiplied, there were rumblings of discontent" (Acts 6:1 NLT). Satan immediately came in to challenge what the Lord had done. As the Lord is blessing a local church or a certain group of believers who are doing His work, divisions sometimes will come from those who want to stir things up. It seems that some people are always mad at someone. Yet the Bible says that among the seven things God hates are "a false witness who speaks lies, and one who sows discord among brethren" (Prov. 6:19). Don't be one of those people the enemy uses to create division.

Jesus said, "Blessed are the peacemakers, for they shall be called sons of God" (Matt. 5:9). I've always found that it is much better to forgive and to let God deal with people.

When we live holy lives,
we will live happy lives as well.

I am not calling for unity at any cost, however. Truth is even more important than unity. But at the same time, we can flex in the nonessentials. It has been said, "In essentials, unity; in nonessentials, liberty; in all things, charity."

Why is our unity so important? Because it stands as a powerful witness to a divided world when we overcome our generational, racial, socioeconomic, and cultural differences and are unified around Christ.

A PRAYER FOR FUTURE BELIEVERS

Finally, Jesus prayed for us and for the ones that we will reach: "I do not pray for these alone, but also for those who will believe in Me through their word" (v. 20). As we live lives that glorify and honor God, as we seek to be holy and set apart for His service, as we love one another, the world will take notice.

So here in John 17, we have seen Jesus' prayer for us and for what He desires in our lives.

First, He desires for us to live lives that glorify Him. That is why we are here. This is why we exist.

Second, He desires our preservation. Even so, He wants our partnership and cooperation in this endeavor. He will keep us saved, but He wants us to keep ourselves safe as we "keep ourselves in the love of God."

Third, He desires our consecration, that we would live sanctified lives, set apart for Him, and that we would seek to be holy before the Lord. At the same time, He wants us to impact our culture, not isolating ourselves, but infiltrating and permeating the world around us.

Fourth, He desires our unity, that we would love one another—not destroy one another. He wants us to overcome our differences, pulling together for what we have in common in Him as a testimony before a lost and divided world.

6 THE PURPOSE IN
GETHSEMANE

John 18:1–11

Have you ever felt lonely? Cut off? Had your friends abandon you? Have you ever been completely misunderstood? Then you have a faint idea of what Jesus went through as He agonized in Gethsemane.

We all will face our Gethsemanes in life, times when it seems as though the whole world is closing in on us. We all will face times of ultimate stress, when the circumstances in which we find ourselves seem too much to bear, when it feels like we can't go on another day.

Jesus has provided a model for us of what to do in times of uncertainty. We don't always know the will of God in every situation. And then there are times when we do know it, but we don't like it. At other times, God's will doesn't make sense, just as it didn't seem to make sense at the time to men like Joseph and Job. Yet we must never be afraid to place an unknown future into the hands of a known God.

It has been said that "ignorance is bliss," and "What you don't know won't hurt you." There is some truth to these statements. After all, Jesus, being God, knew full well what horrors awaited Him in just a few, short hours when He would go to a Roman cross to be crucified. This would take place after a time of humiliation, beating, and horrendous whipping.

Jesus has been there,
and He is there for you.

Here in this unique and insightful portion of Scripture, we are given a rare, behind-the-scenes look at the personal struggles of Jesus as He contemplated the cup He had to drink. The Bible says that He was "a Man of sorrows and acquainted with grief" (Isa. 53:3). But the sorrow Jesus experienced in Gethsemane on the night before His crucifixion seemed to be the culmination of all the sorrow He had ever known. And it would accelerate to a climax the following day. We cannot even begin to grasp the anguish Jesus experienced at that moment, because being omniscient, He was fully aware of what lay ahead.

Jesus' time in Gethsemane, next to the cross itself, was the loneliest moment of His life. We need to remember this in our moments of loneliness when feel that our friends have abandoned us or that our family—or perhaps even God—has let us down. Jesus has been there, and He is there for you. He knows what you are going through. Hebrews 4:15–16 offers this promise: "For we do not have a High Priest who cannot sympathize with our weaknesses, but was in all points tempted as we are, yet without sin. Let us therefore come boldly to the throne of grace, that we may obtain mercy and find grace to help in time of need."

When we are facing our own Gethsemanes, when life is not making any sense, when problems seem too great to bear, when we are seemingly overwhelmed, there is a point in which we have to say something that is very important to God. And here in John 18, we will discover what that is.

Much is said about the cross, and rightly so. But here in the Garden of Gethsemane, we see how agonizingly the decision was made that took Jesus to the cross. The ultimate triumph that would take place at Calvary was first accomplished beneath the gnarled, old olive trees of Gethsemane. None of the wonderful things Jesus promised during His ministry would have materialized if the events recorded here in John 18 had not first taken place. The promise of eternal life, the sending of the Holy Spirit as Comforter, Jesus' return for His church— all were dependent on what happened on the cross and on His resurrection.

Through this glimpse of Jesus in Gethsemane, I hope we find a greater appreciation for all He has done for us. The apostle Paul declared, "The life which I now live in the flesh I live by faith in the Son of God, who loved me and gave Himself for me" (Gal. 2:20). Our love for Him should grow as we learn more about His love for us.

FROM EDEN TO GETHSEMANE

It all happened in a garden. I find it interesting that sin began in a garden, and the commitment to bear that sin also took place in one. In Eden, Adam and Eve sinned; in Gethsemane, Jesus conquered. In Eden, Adam and Eve hid themselves; in Gethsemane, our Lord boldly presented himself. In Eden, the sword was drawn; in Gethsemane, it was sheathed.

———◦◦◦◦———

*Our love for Him should grow as we
learn more about His love for us.*

———◦◦◦◦———

At this point in His life, Jesus had preached His
last public sermon and had eaten His last meal with
the Twelve. He had prayed a beautiful prayer for
His disciples—past, present, and future. And now,
the final events in His journey toward the cross
begin to unfold:

> When Jesus had spoken these words, He
> went out with His disciples over the Brook
> Kidron, where there was a garden, which He
> and His disciples entered. And Judas, who
> betrayed Him, also knew the place; for Jesus
> often met there with His disciples. (vv. 1–2)

Between verses 1 and 2, there is a chronological
gap, which the other Gospels fill in for us.
Matthew's Gospel tells us that Jesus then said to
Peter, James, and John, "Stay here and watch with
Me" (Matt. 26:38). The conventional thinking
surrounding these three disciples is that Jesus
probably singled them out because they were
ultraspiritual. But let me offer another possibility.

When I was in school, I would often get into
trouble. As a result, my teacher would have me
sit at the front of the classroom, where it would
be easier to keep an eye on me. We often put
the apostles on pedestals, but the Bible portrays
them honestly, warts and all. Peter's *faux pas*
are legendary. James and John were a couple of
firebrands too. Remember, they did not acquire
their nickname, "Sons of Thunder," for nothing.
When one Samaritan village wasn't receptive to
Jesus' ministry, it was James and John who said,
"Lord, do You want us to command fire to come
down from heaven and consume them, just as
Elijah did?" (Luke 9:54). Jesus rebuked them and
said, "You do not know what manner of spirit you
are of. For the Son of Man did not come to destroy
men's lives but to save them" (vv. 55–56). So as
Jesus' hour approached, perhaps He just wanted
"The Rock" and "The Thunder Boys" nearby.

THE NEED FOR COMPANIONSHIP

All Jesus asked was that they stay there and watch
with Him. Imagine that! What an honor it was!
Jesus didn't say, "Explain this to Me," because He
didn't need an explanation. He didn't say, "Preach

to Me," because He didn't need a sermon. Rather, to these three, privileged disciples, He simply said, "Stay with Me." Jesus, who was God yet human, was experiencing intense loneliness.

Sometimes the best thing we can do for someone who is suffering is to simply be there. The Bible tells us to "Bear one another's burdens, and so fulfill the law of Christ" (Gal. 6:2). When Job's entire world fell apart, and everything he held dear in life was stripped away, his wife said, "Curse God and die!" Now wouldn't that make a nice greeting card to send to someone who is hurting? What Job really needed was some encouragement. So when Job's three friends came to visit, and upon seeing his miserable condition and his body covered with boils, they were so stunned that they simply wept with him. Then they sat with him for seven days without saying a word. And guess what? That was the perfect thing to do, because the Bible tells us to "weep with those who weep" (Rom. 12:15).

As a young preacher, this truth came as a revelation to me. I always had the quick answer or the clever statement, especially at age 21. But then I came to realize that even though there are certainly times for that, there are also times to simply be there for someone, especially when they are suffering. It's been said that we should "Preach the gospel at all times, and when necessary, use words." We must avoid the easy answers and clichés when we're attempting to comfort suffering people. We should avoid saying, "I know how you feel," when we really don't. We should avoid suggesting, "There's a reason for everything," when we really can't see one. We should avoid blurting out, "Cheer up, there is always someone worse off," when the one who is suffering can always see someone who is better off.

Jesus, who was God yet human, was experiencing intense loneliness.

So why did Jesus desire the companionship of Peter, James, and John here in Gethsemane? Because He was in agony. Jesus told them, "My soul is exceedingly sorrowful, even to death … " (Matt. 26:38). Mark's Gospel adds this detail: "Going a little farther, he fell to the ground and prayed that if possible the hour might pass from him" (Mark 14:35 NIV). Evidently, Jesus was in such agony that He would cast himself to the ground, then stand up, then again fall to the ground in prayer.

THE CUP HE WOULD DRINK

In one of the most dramatic descriptions of Jesus' suffering in Gethsemane, Luke writes,

> And He was withdrawn from them about a stone's throw, and He knelt down and prayed, saying, "Father, if it is Your will, take this cup away from Me; nevertheless not My will, but Yours, be done." Then an angel appeared to Him from heaven, strengthening Him. (Luke 22:41–43)

Jesus, being God, knew the future. He knew He would be denied by the one in whom he had invested the most: Simon Peter. He knew that He would become the object of Peter's shame and the cause of his cursing. He knew He would be rejected by His people Israel, whom He had come to save: "He came to His own, and His own did not receive Him" (John 1:11). He had wept over their very unbelief, and now He would witness it in full force. He knew that His disciples Judas Iscariot, whom He loved, was about to betray Him with a kiss. He knew He would be vilified in a kangaroo court of injustice and subjected to unfair treatment, ironically all in the name of God. But worst of all, He who had been in constant communion with the Father and the Holy Spirit would find himself forsaken by the Father as He became sin for the whole world. This is why He prayed, "My Father, if it is possible, may this cup be taken from me … " (Matt. 26:39 NIV).

It was the fact that He who was holy, righteous, and pure was to take upon himself all that was unholy, unrighteous, and impure. He was about to bear every vile, perverse sin of humanity. Everything in His thirty-three years on Earth had been building to this event. From the moment of His birth, Jesus lived in the shadow of the cross. From the moment the prophet Simeon told Mary, "A sword will pierce through your own soul…" (Luke 2:35), it was clear that Jesus was destined to die—and not only die, but die under the wrath of God.

Jesus began to aggressively address the subject from Caesarea Philippi: "From that time Jesus began to show to His disciples that He must go to Jerusalem, and suffer many things from the elders and chief priests and scribes, and be killed, and be raised the third day" (Matt. 16:21). Jesus knew exactly what lay ahead. But He dreaded taking the sin upon himself, as well as experiencing even temporary separation from the Father. Even during those grueling moments, we will see that He remained in unbroken communion with His Father, though temporarily eclipsed as He cried out, "My God, My God, why have You forsaken Me?" (Matt. 27:46). Jesus had come to "taste death for everyone" (Heb. 2:9). As Alfred Edersheim wrote, "He disarmed Death by burying his shaft in His own Heart."[1]

From the moment of His birth, Jesus lived in the shadow of the cross.

In Mark's Gospel the first recorded words of Jesus' prayer were, "Abba, Father … " (Mark 14:36), the affectionate cry of a child. He was confident in His Father's will and direction. Yet there was this struggle, which Jesus referred to as "this cup." What was "this cup" He recoiled from? Isaiah called it "the cup of His fury" (Isa. 51:17). Have you ever tasted something that turned your stomach? Imagine having to drink it all down. That is what Jesus had to do. He had to drink "this cup." On one occasion, the mother of James and John came to Jesus with an ambitious request: "In your Kingdom, will you let my two sons sit in places of honor next to you, one at your right and the other at your left?" (Matt. 20:21 NLT).

So He asked James and John, "Are you able to drink from the bitter cup of sorrow I am about to drink?" (v. 22 NLT).

Jesus indeed drank that cup. He made that final sacrifice, saying to the Father, "Nevertheless, not what I will, but what You will" (Mark 14:36).

Luke offers additional insight into what Jesus was going through in Gethsemane: "And being in agony, He prayed more earnestly. Then His sweat became like great drops of blood falling down to the ground" (Luke 22:24). Dr. Luke is the only one who mentions this detail. It may be that Luke was describing the fact that Jesus' sweat had become so thick and concentrated, it was like blood dropping to the ground. There is a rare phenomenon known as hematridrosis (or hemihidrosis), in which a body is under such emotional stress that the tiny blood vessels in the sweat glands rupture and produce a mixture of blood and sweat. Clearly Jesus was under incredible spiritual and physical strain at this moment. And I have no doubt that the devil was there in full force as well. We know that he had already entered the heart of Judas (see John 13:2), who was in the garden and approaching.

But from the biblical accounts of Jesus' coming back to the disciples three times, we might conclude that He was facing waves of temptation, similar to what He faced during His temptation in the wilderness. The temptation that He was facing, most likely, was not to go to the cross. The devil had tried this on Him before, offering Jesus all the kingdoms of the world if Jesus would just worship him (see Matt. 4:8–9). Satan was essentially offering Jesus a shortcut around the cross. But Jesus would have nothing to do with it, not then, and not now. He knew there was only one way to settle this sin issue. He had to taste death for everyone. He had to drink the cup. He had to go to the cross and die for our sins.

It is insulting to God to suggest that all religions are true.

This is why it is insulting to God to suggest that all religions are true, and that Jesus is just one of many ways to God. If that were true, do you think God the Father would have allowed Jesus to go through this? For Jesus, it was a fate worse than death.

THE JOY SET BEFORE HIM

So what was it that kept Him moving forward, in spite of the fact that He was about to face excruciating pain and torture and be forsaken by His own followers? What was it that caused Him to go through this, knowing that even the Father would momentarily forsake Him as He took upon himself the sin of the world? We find the answer in Hebrews 12:

> Therefore we also, since we are surrounded by so great a cloud of witnesses, let us lay aside every weight, and the sin which so easily ensnares us, and let us run with endurance the race that is set before us, looking unto Jesus, the author and finisher of our faith, who for the joy that was set before Him endured the cross, despising the shame, and has sat down at the right hand of the throne of God. (Heb. 12:1–2)

Unwittingly, Peter was playing right into the hands of the enemy.

What is that "joy" verse 2 speaks of? Jesus told the story of a shepherd who had a lamb that went astray. The shepherd went and found the lamb and brought it back, wrapped around his shoulders. Jesus then said, "Likewise there will be more joy in heaven over one sinner who repents than over ninety-nine just persons who need no repentance" (Luke 15:8). *We* are that joy.

Jesus also told a parable about hidden treasure, saying, "The kingdom of heaven is like treasure hidden in a field. When a man found it, he hid it again, and then in his joy went and sold all he had and bought that field" (Matt. 13:44 NIV). *We* are that treasure, that reason He went through this pain and agony.

NOT A VICTIM, BUT A VICTOR

Now the multitude was pressing in, led by the wicked Judas. Matthew tells us this was a large crowd (see Matt. 26:47), which would have included the temple "police," as well as a cohort of Roman soldiers, which at full strength numbered six hundred. Altogether, about one thousand armed people probably came to arrest one individual with His eleven peaceful disciples. And here came Judas, with the temple guard in tow:

Then Judas, having received a detachment
of troops, and officers from the chief priests
and Pharisees, came there with lanterns,
torches, and weapons. Jesus therefore,
knowing all things that would come upon
Him, went forward and said to them,
"Whom are you seeking?" They answered
Him, Jesus of Nazareth." Jesus said to them,
"I am He." (vv. 3–5)

Rather than falling back, Jesus stepped toward
them, asking "Whom are you seeking?" Then John
tells us, "And Judas, who betrayed Him, also stood
with them. Now when He said to them, 'I am He,'
they drew back and fell to the ground" (vv. 5–6).

Jesus was using His divine title as God. When
Moses was called by God, the Lord identified
himself as "I AM." Jesus' response here in
Gethsemane was the last exercise of His power
by which He calmed the seas, stilled the winds,
and healed the sick. Undoubtedly, He was not a
hapless victim, but a powerful victor who could
have easily gotten out of this situation. He was
warning them all that they were in way over their
heads. He could have called on thousands of angels
or could have simply spoken these people out of
existence: "I AM … and you *were*! Bye!" And poof,

they all could have been gone. But remember, Jesus said, "Therefore My Father loves Me, because I lay down My life that I may take it again. No one takes it from Me, but I lay it down of Myself. I have power to lay it down, and I have power to take it again. This command I have received from My Father" (John 10:17–18).

Judas then betrayed Him with a kiss. This truly was a kiss from hell. Why a kiss? Why not simply point at Jesus? Because Judas was the hypocrite extraordinaire. Even in this, the hour of ultimate betrayal, he wanted to appear to be spiritual. This is almost like a sickness, to want to look good on the outside when you are diseased on the inside.

Peter is fuming as he watches this and decides to try and save the day:

> Then Simon Peter, having a sword, drew it and struck the high priest's servant, and cut off his right ear. The servant's name was Malchus. So Jesus said to Peter, "Put your sword into the sheath. Shall I not drink the cup which My Father has given Me?"
> (vv. 10–11)

On one hand, we want to commend Peter for his act of bravery, but on the other hand, Jesus did not condone this and told Peter to put his sword away. Poor Peter. He just couldn't get it right. He was boasting when he should have been listening, and sleeping when he should have been praying. Now he was fighting when he should have been surrendering. This was pure stupidity on Peter's part. He wasn't thinking; he was reacting—as if Jesus could not have escaped this with one word to heaven! Peter seemed to be an emotional man, given to the impulse of the moment.

Preaching the gospel and praying are two of the most powerful weapons in our spiritual arsenal.

In addition to telling him to put away his sword, Jesus told Peter, "Those who use the sword will be killed by the sword. Don't you realize that I could ask my Father for thousands of angels to protect us, and he would send them instantly?" (Matt. 26:52–53 NLT). I can imagine that even those angels were waiting with swords drawn, ready for the word from Jesus.

WRONG ENEMY, WRONG WEAPON

When Peter pulled out his sword and struck the servant of the high priest, he made the same mistake that we often make. He was fighting the wrong enemy with the wrong weapon. Our enemies are not flesh and blood, and they cannot be defeated with ordinary weapons: "We are human, but we don't wage war with human plans and methods. We use God's mighty weapons, not mere worldly weapons, to knock down the Devil's strongholds (2 Cor. 10:3–4 NLT).

Preaching the gospel and praying are two of the most powerful weapons in our spiritual arsenal. Some Christians get very excited about picketing and boycotting, and there may be a place for that. But often it draws more attention to the thing that is being picketed. I remember when the Martin Scorsese film, *The Last Temptation of Christ*, was released, triggering a great outcry from the church. The film was picketed, and ticket sales went up. But then the church returned the favor when Mel Gibson produced *The Passion of the Christ*. There were charges that it was allegedly anti-Semitic, among other things, yet it was one of the top-grossing films in Hollywood history.

My point is that it is more effective to turn on the light than to curse the darkness. That is why evangelism is so important.

ONE FINAL MIRACLE

So Peter, in an impulsive moment, cuts off the ear of Malchus. Jesus stopped him, and then stooped down to heal the man's injury. Amid this flurry of activity in the garden, very few noticed the last miracle of Jesus' earthly ministry. It wasn't a big, flashy, go-out-with-a-bang miracle, but a quiet one. This final miracle showed His true heart. He healed the ear of one of the first people who came to arrest Him. He received no thanks from this man that we know of. Yet as He faced this lynch mob, Jesus hadn't forgotten about the needs of an individual. And hours later on the cross, He would be praying for the forgiveness of the men who were crucifying Him.

It's also worth noting that the last miracle Jesus performed was made necessary by a blundering disciple. Jesus probably has been busy healing the wounds made by blundering disciples ever since, maybe even some of mine or some of yours.

*It is more effective to turn on the light
than to curse the darkness.*

FACING OUR GETHSEMANES

Yes, we all will face our Gethsemanes in life.
Therefore, we would do well to remember these
words from the apostle Paul: "Let this mind be
in you which was also in Christ Jesus …" (Phil
2:5). Jesus prayed, "Not as I will, but as You will"
(Matt. 26:39), and every one of us must come to
this point. We all will face times of ultimate stress
in which the cup we must drink appears to be too
much for us. It is then that we must say the one
thing God wants to hear each of His children say:
"Not as I will, but as You will!" I like the advice of
D. L. Moody, who said, "Spread out your petition
before God, and then say, 'Thy will, not mine, be
done.' The sweetest lesson I have learned in God's
school is to let the Lord choose for me." Would
you be willing to take your future, place it into
God's hands, and let Him choose for you? There
comes a point where we must say, "Lord, I don't
get what is happening to me right now, but I

trust You completely and say, 'Not as I will, but as You will.' "

I came across a poem that expresses well what our mindset should be when we face our Gethsemanes:

> All those who journey, soon or late, Must pass within the garden's gate; Must kneel alone in darkness there, And battle with some fierce despair. God pity those who cannot say, "Not mine, but Thine," who only pray, "Let this cup pass," and cannot see The purpose in Gethsemane. ... [2]

There was a purpose in Gethsemane for Jesus ... and for us as well. It is a place where we realize obedience overrules personal desire, where Spirit becomes more important than flesh, and where the glory of God is more important than our own glory and desires.

Jesus said, "Whoever loses his life for my sake will find it" (Matt. 10:39 NIV), and "Take My yoke upon you and learn from Me, for I am gentle and lowly in heart, and you will find rest for your souls" (Matt. 11:29). So don't be afraid to pray, "Abba, Father" and surrender yourself to His perfect will for your life. He has your best interests in mind. His plans, His purpose, and His future for you

INDECISION

John 18:12–13; 19–40

We've all experienced it at one time or another, some more so than others. It's called indecision. Most of the time, I am pretty decisive. But then there are those times when I simply can't decide, like when I go into certain restaurants and their menus are pages long.

Even some drive-through places have too many choices now. There are burgers, fries, Mexican food, chicken, and even pizza. Then there is the pressure of all the cars lined up behind you, giving you a split second to process the menu before a distorted voice comes through the speaker and asks for your order. That's why I like a drive-through place we have here in Southern California called In-N-Out Burger. The choices are burgers, fries, and beverages, period.

But in the long run, it's really not all that important whether you have a burger or a burrito for lunch. There are other choices that are far more important, such as your career choice, or even more important, the person you will marry. And the most important choice of all is what you will do with Jesus Christ.

———✦———

When we stand before God, it will be a "Son question"–not a "Sin question."

———✦———

We are about to look at the story of an indecisive man, someone who let others do the thinking for him, who tried to appease a bloodthirsty, fickle crowd and his own troubled conscience. He tried to find middle ground and make everyone happy. His name was Pontius Pilate.

Like the indecisive Civil War soldier who tried to play it safe by dressing in a blue coat and gray pants and came under fire from both directions, the indecisive person tries to maintain moral neutrality by insisting there are two sides to every issue. And that is true. But it's also true that there are two sides to a sheet of flypaper. It makes a big difference to the fly as to which side he chooses.

Pilate definitely landed on the wrong side of the flypaper, so to speak, and it was a decision that he no doubt regretted for the rest of his life. In spite of his position of great power, Pilate had to answer a question that we all must eventually come to grips with: "What am I going to do with Jesus?" No one is excused, because on that final day when we stand before God, it will be a "Son question"—not a "Sin question."

This is important to know, because the conventional thinking is that if we are "good," then we will get into heaven, but if we are really "bad," then we will go to hell. The truth is that even someone who has lived a wicked life, but repents in the end, will go to heaven. And someone who has lived a "good," moral life, yet does not repent, will go to hell. No one is ever—or will be—good enough to get into heaven, but because of Jesus, we can go there. But if we reject His offer of forgiveness, then we cannot.

WHEN GOD WENT ON TRIAL

When you get down to it, this is not the story of Jesus before Pilate as much as it is the story of Pilate before Jesus. At this point, Jesus already had been cruelly beaten and rushed through a hastily prepared appearance before the religious elite of the day, the Jewish Sanhedrin. One wonders how these religious leaders could become so corrupt that they would actually try, convict, and execute God in human form. Even if they didn't accept Jesus as their Messiah, why their venomous hatred toward Him and the desire for such a quick execution?

It is the same reason people today reject Jesus Christ without even taking the time to consider His claims. They won't even read the Bible, yet they reject it wholesale. They refuse to even listen to someone proclaim the gospel. Why not, simply in the name of fairness, listen to the essential message of the gospel? It is because they don't want to change their lifestyle or their ways, as John 3:19 tells us: "This is the verdict: Light has come into the world, but men loved darkness instead of light because their deeds were evil. Everyone who does evil hates the light, and will not come into the light for fear that his deeds will be exposed" (John 3:19 NLT).

In the minds of the religious leaders, Jesus was bad for business. He had blown their cover, and they wanted to get rid of Him. The fact of the matter is that all of it was playing right into the will and plan of God. As we look at this first-century legal system, we see how justice was miscarried. But it was, in fact, a very fair and just system when properly administered.

Certainly our legal and judicial system is in need of an overhaul. We are too lenient on criminals, and justice is far from swift. There are far too many frivolous lawsuits and too many judges who are liberal and loose when it comes to doing what is right. The further we have drifted from the biblical foundation on which we built our judicial system, the progressively weaker it has become.

They wanted Pilate to do their dirty work.

In the days of first-century Israel, it was different—at least initially. The general requirements of fairness and impartiality prescribed in Deuteronomy 16:18–20 and elsewhere in the Mosaic law were reflected in the rabbinical requirements that guaranteed an accused criminal the right to a public trial, to defense counsel, and conviction only on the testimony of at least two reliable witnesses. Trials, therefore, were always open to public scrutiny, and the defendant had the right to bring forth evidence and witnesses on his own behalf, no matter how damning the evidence and testimony against him might be. To prevent false testimony being given in a court of law, whether given out of revenge or for a bribe, the Mosaic law prescribed that one who knowingly gave false testimony would suffer the same punishment the accused would suffer if he or she were found guilty (Deut. 19:16–19). So, for example, if you were found to have given false testimony in a trial that resulted in the death penalty for the accused, then you would be put to death as well. Needless to say, this was a strong deterrent against perjury.

Pilate was unnerved at Jesus' calmness in the face of His own death.

In addition, there was always to be a presumption of innocence. If the accused was found innocent, he was freed immediately. If the accused was found guilty, however, the sentence was not pronounced until two days later. In addition, the council members also were required to fast during the intervening day. On the morning of the third day, the council was called together, and each judge, in turn, was asked if he had changed his decision. If a guilty verdict was reaffirmed, an officer with a flag remained near the council, while another officer, often mounted on horseback, escorted the prisoner to the place of execution. A herald went out before the slow-moving procession, declaring in a loud voice that the person was being led to punishment. The prisoner's crime was stated, the witnesses against him were named, and a final invitation was issued: "If anyone has evidence to give in his favor, let him come forward quickly." If, at any time before the sentence was carried out, additional information pertaining to the prisoner's innocence came to light, including the prisoner's recollection of something he had forgotten, one officer would signal the other, and the prisoner would be brought back to the council for reconsideration of the verdict. The governing principle in capital cases was, "The Sanhedrin is to save, not destroy, life."

No criminal trial could be begun during, or continued into, the night. The property of an executed criminal could not be confiscated, but was passed to his heirs, and voting was done from the youngest member to the oldest so the former wouldn't be influenced by the latter.

Sadly, all these principles were ignored the night of Jesus' arrest. He was illegally tried without first having been charged with a crime. He was tried at night and in private, and He wasn't permitted a defense. The witnesses against Him had been bribed to falsify their testimonies, and He was executed on the same day He was sentenced. The judges obviously could not have fasted, because there was no intervening day between the trial and the sentence, and they had no opportunity to reconsider their verdict. It was a complete and unequivocal travesty of justice.

Before they took Jesus to Caiaphas' house, he was first taken to the house of his father-in-law, Annas (see vv. 12–13). Some twenty years earlier, Annas had served as high priest for a period of four or five years. And although he had been replaced as a ruling high priest, he was a godfather figure of sorts to the others, continuing to wield great influence in temple affairs. Annas was the first to question Jesus:

> The high priest then asked Jesus about His disciples and His doctrine. Jesus answered him, "I spoke openly to the world. I always

taught in synagogues and in the temple,
where the Jews always meet, and in secret
I have said nothing. Why do you ask Me?
Ask those who have heard Me what I said to
them. Indeed they know what I said." And
when He had said these things, one of the
officers who stood by struck Jesus with the
palm of his hand, saying, "Do You answer
the high priest like that?" (vv. 19–22)

Jesus was then taken, bound, to Caiaphas, who
accused the Lord of blasphemy. Mark's Gospel
tells us, "Then some began to spit on Him, and to
blindfold Him, and to beat Him, and to say to Him,
'Prophesy!' And the officers struck Him with the
palms of their hands." (Mark 14:65).

Undeniably, there was a lot of pent-up hostility
toward Christ. His very life and ministry exposed
their religious hypocrisy. His most scathing words
were reserved for them and their ilk. Pilate later
observed they wanted Him dead because of envy.
But they didn't want to personally kill Jesus; rather,
they wanted Pilate to do it for them.

THE HORNS OF A DILEMMA

So they brought Jesus to Pontius Pilate. Pilate
immediately found himself on the horns of a

dilemma—a quandary. It was the time of the Jewish Passover, and the city swelled with pilgrims. Pilate did not want these religious rulers inciting a riot against him. Things were already tense, after all. Pilate was the Roman governor, or procurator, of Judea. Governors in this time were not elected by the people, but were appointed by Rome, the ruling power. Pilate was one of the many regional representatives who reported to Rome. Normally, Pilate would have been kicking back at his beautiful palace on the Mediterranean coast in Caesarea, but he had to be in Jerusalem during Passover week, because the crowds were so large.

If Pilate had opened his heart, he would have realized that he was standing before Truth Incarnate.

At this time, Pilate was already in hot water with Rome. He had already had a number of run-ins with the Jews, whom he hated. In a letter written to Caligula, the emperor who succeeded Tiberias, Agrippa delivered a scathing testimony regarding Pilate: "Pilate is unbending and recklessly hard. He is a man of notorious reputation, severe brutality, prejudice, savage violence, and murder." As a result, Pilate was "on report." He was being investigated by Rome. The emperor had ordered surveillance of this governor after reading these reports about him. This is why the otherwise unbending, brutal, prejudicial Pilate appeared so vacillating and indecisive in his dealings with Jesus. And this explains why he did not throw the Jews out of the palace when they came asking for Jesus' death. Pilate was scared, plain and simple. This hardened, anti-Semitic Roman cared nothing about public opinion. It's just that it was his head in the noose, so he had to keep the Jews from rioting to prevent Rome from turning on him. I think Pilate would have otherwise freed Jesus, just to spite the Jews, not to mention that Jesus was innocent. And I believe, in his heart of hearts, that Pilate realized it.

A MEANS TO AN END

This was the man who would decide the fate of the Son of God. But that day, there was more taking place than met the eye. The forces of good and evil were at work. Both God and Satan were mysteriously moving in the same direction, but

with very different objectives. Satan wanted Jesus
dead, and so he gathered his forces and played
his wicked hand. God wanted the sin of the world
dealt with, and that would only happen through the
death of His Son.

It wasn't that Pilate had no choice in the matter.
He would have to make a decision concerning Jesus
Christ. But, as he was about to discover,
he had no easy way out:

> Then they led Jesus from Caiaphas to the
> Praetorium, and it was early morning.
> But they themselves did not go into the
> Praetorium, lest they should be defiled, but
> that they might eat the Passover. Pilate then
> went out to them and said, "What accusation
> do you bring against this Man?" (vv. 28–29)

Revealing the complete sham of their so-called
"faith," the Jewish leaders didn't want to go into
Pilate's headquarters for fear they would be defiled,
yet they were in a rush to crucify an innocent man,
which was against everything the Torah stood for.
These religious leaders really wanted Pilate to
do their dirty work for them, without even
examining Jesus.

So Pilate asked, "What are the charges
against this Man?"

As though their dignity were being impugned, they retorted, "We wouldn't have handed him over to you if he weren't a criminal!"

"Take Him yourselves and judge Him according to your law, … " Pilate told them.

Pilate was, in essence, giving them permission to execute Jesus, because he knew that according to their laws, the most serious religious offenders were punishable by death. Their design, however, was not simply to have Jesus put to death, but to avoid responsibility for it, as well as possible reprisals from their own people. What they wanted was a Roman execution, and they wanted Pilate to do their dirty work. Not only were they wicked, but they were cowards as well: "It is not lawful for us to put anyone to death" (v. 31).

Satan, working through the Jewish leaders (regardless of their motives), was playing into God's hands. By demanding a Roman crucifixion instead of stoning, which was the Jews' usual practice, these religious leaders unwittingly made certain the prophecy of Psalm 22 would be fulfilled: "They pierced My hands and My feet" (Ps. 22:16).

Then there were Jesus' own repeated references as to what kind of death He would die. Jesus told

His disciples earlier, "When we get to Jerusalem…
the Son of Man will be betrayed to the leading
priests and the teachers of religious law. They
will sentence him to die. Then they will hand him
over to the Romans to be mocked, whipped, and
crucified. But on the third day he will be raised
from the dead" (Matt. 20:18–19 NLT).

PILATE BEFORE JESUS

By the time Jesus was brought to Pilate, He already
had been beaten. No doubt with a touch of satire,
Pilate exclaimed, "Are You the King of the Jews?"

*Jesus was a political hot potato,
and Pilate had a career to think about.*

In his position, Pilate had pretty much seen it
all. All criminal penalties in Judea were subject to
Pilate's ultimate approval or veto, either directly
or indirectly through courts that operated under
his oversight. He had presided over hundreds,
perhaps thousands of criminal proceedings.
All of the accused, of course, would have
protested their innocence.

A story is told about Frederick the Great, King of Prussia, who visited a prison and talked with each of the inmates. There he heard endless tales of innocence, of misunderstood motives, and of exploitation. When the king stopped at the cell of a man who remained silent, he said to the prisoner, "Well, I suppose you are an innocent victim too?"

The man replied, "No, Sir, I am not. I'm guilty and deserve my punishment."

Turning to the warden, the king said, "Here, release this rascal before he corrupts all these fine, innocent people in here!"

In contrast to that prisoner, Jesus did not profess guilt or innocence. He just stood there and took it. Pilate had never met anyone who was obviously innocent, yet really did nothing to speak in His own defense. Pilate was unnerved at Jesus' calmness in the face of His own death.

" 'You say that I am a king, and you are right,' Jesus said. 'I was born for that purpose. And I came to bring truth to the world. All who love the truth recognize that what I say is true' " (v. 37 NLT).

"What is truth?" Pilate callously responded. Pilate was a pagan man who had no core beliefs other than self–preservation. His descendents

today would be identified as moral relativists
or postmodernists, those who insist that truth
is a matter of subjective opinion. They doubt
everything and distrust everything, attaching
bumper stickers to their cars (next to their
Darwin fish symbols) that say, "Question
Authority." Amazingly, this ideology not only
has been taught in our major universities for
decades, but has been embraced by many,
if not most. Research has indicated that 67 percent
of Americans do not believe in absolute truth.

If Pilate had only opened his heart, he would
have realized that he was standing before Truth
Incarnate. But this jaded Roman governor
just wanted this entire escapade over with. He
desperately wanted out of this situation, as many
people do when they are confronted with the truth
of the gospel. Maybe you've known people like this.
When you start telling them about Jesus, they try
to change the subject, leave the room, barrage you
with tough questions, and do anything but listen
carefully to what you are saying. The Holy Spirit,
doing His work of conviction, is the reason for their
discomfort. This was the case with Pilate.

It's not that he disliked Jesus. In fact, he seemed

to admire Him. But Jesus was a political hot potato, and Pilate had a career to think about. He was looking for a way out, and then it came to him. Pilate heard that Jesus was from Galilee, which was under his rival Herod's jurisdiction. So Pilate shuffled Jesus off to Herod, hoping never to see him again. But you can't get rid of Jesus—or your need to make a decision about Him.

You can't get rid of Jesus—or your need to make a decision about Him.

Herod welcomed Jesus not because he believed in Him, but because he was hoping to see a miracle. Not only did Herod fail to see a miracle, but he didn't even have the privilege of hearing Jesus' voice. Little did Herod know that Jesus' silence was fulfilling another important prophecy regarding the Messiah: "He was oppressed and treated harshly, yet he never said a word. He was led as a lamb to the slaughter. And as a sheep is silent before the shearers, he did not open his mouth" (Isa. 53:7 NLT). Responsible for the death of John the Baptist, Herod had an irreparably hardened heart. And showing his true colors, he mocked Jesus, arrayed him in a "kingly" robe, and sent him back to Pilate.

Pilate once again was forced to deal with Jesus. But suddenly he had an idea. It was the ultimate compromise. There was a custom among the Jews to release a prisoner at Passover. He would offer Barabbas, who was largely hated, and Jesus, who still had His supporters. Barabbas was a wicked man who tried to lead a revolt against Rome. He was tried and convicted of robbery, sedition, and murder. This clever strategy would surely get Pilate off the hook. It would enable him to release Jesus, which he clearly wanted to do, without defying the will of the Sanhedrin, whom he did not want to offend at this time. He could simply argue that he was carrying out the will of the people. It really was a brilliant diplomatic maneuver. Of course the people wouldn't choose the release of a man like Barabbas over someone like Jesus! Or so he thought.

So Pilate posed his question to the religious leaders:

> "But you have a custom that I should release someone to you at the Passover. Do you therefore want me to release to you the King of the Jews?" Then they all cried

again, saying, "Not this Man, but Barabbas!"
Now Barabbas was a robber. (vv. 39–40)

---

*Pilate listened to the wrong voice
and made the wrong decision.*

The religious leaders had already infiltrated
the fickle crowds and convinced them to demand the release of Barabbas. These were the
same crowds who, only days earlier, had cried,
"Hosanna! Blessed is He who comes in the name
of the Lord!" (see John 12:13). There also were, no
doubt, those who hated Jesus for what He said and
stood for. As Jesus said to Pilate, "All who love the
truth recognize that what I say is true" (v. 37).
But most did not love Jesus or the truth. They
loved Him as long as He filled their empty
stomachs or healed their sick. But once He had
served their purpose, they had no perceived need
or interest in Him.

A WIFE'S WARNING

Matthew fills in some gaps for us here: "While
he [Pilate] was sitting on the judgment seat, his

wife sent to him, saying, 'Have nothing to do with that just Man, for I have suffered many things today in a dream because of Him' " (Matt. 27:19). This sounded like more than a woman's intuition (although a wise man will learn to listen to his wife). It seems this may have been a God-given dream. The Bible says that Pilate's wife "suffered many things … in a dream because of Him," but it is not clear what she meant by that. Had she been brought face-to-face with her own sins? One thing was clear to her: Jesus was both right and innocent. Her counsel to Pilate was, "Have nothing to do with that just Man."

Undoubtedly Pilate knew what path he should take, but again, this was about career and position and power—all very powerful elements in a man's life. It's from these very things that most men find their purpose. When meeting for the first time, it's usually a matter of minutes before men ask each other, "So, what do you do for a living?" Pilate had worked long and hard to get to this position, and he did not want to lose it. Still, he had within his power the ability to pardon Jesus:

> But the chief priests and elders persuaded the multitudes that they should ask for Barabbas and destroy Jesus. The governor

answered and said to them, "Which of the two do you want me to release to you?" They said, "Barabbas!" Pilate said to them, "What then shall I do with Jesus who is called Christ?" They all said to him, "Let Him be crucified!" (Matt. 27:20–23)

The meaning of "Barabbas" is significant: "Son of the father." In fact, it's a title, not a name. One or two of the ancient manuscripts gives his name as "Jesus Barabbas," the very name and title of our Lord. Many self-proclaimed Messiahs had arisen at this time in history, making Messianic claims and calling themselves "Barabbas." Therefore, this Barabbas may have been presenting himself as the Messiah, which makes the crowd's choice all the more appalling. The way Pilate worded his question suggests that Barabbas' first name was Jesus. Otherwise, why would Pilate ask, "What then shall I do with Jesus *who is called Christ?*" (Matt. 20:22, emphasis mine). Pilate was contrasting Him with the other Jesus, called Barabbas, essentially saying, "You are choosing Jesus, called Barabbas. What shall I do with Jesus called Christ?" They were required to choose between a man who led a rebellion and committed murder and a man against whom not one charge of violence could be brought.

Behind their choice was a false perception of the kingdom, of a new government that would come by force. Yet as Jesus said to Pilate, "My kingdom is not of this world. If My kingdom were of this world, My servants would fight … " (v. 36). However, these people would have none of it. They screamed for the release of Barabbas and the crucifixion of Jesus.

A LAST-DITCH EFFORT

The multitude clearly wanted blood, not justice. And even to the hardened, pagan mind of Pilate, their vicious response must have been blood-chilling. So Pilate attempted another compromise, in spite of his failed attempt to turn Jesus over to Herod or to release Jesus in keeping with the custom at Passover time. Pilate took water, washed his hands, and declared, "I am innocent of the blood of this just Person. You see to it" (Matt. 27:20).

This is so typical of many today. They want to just put off what they don't want to deal with. But you cannot put off certain things, even if you want to. And one of those "things" is Jesus. Pilate could have done the right thing and not allowed this.

Instead, he did was politically expedient and what would advance his career. He took the path of least resistance—and also the path that damned his soul.

<hr>

Most did not love Jesus or the truth.

<hr>

Scripture is clear in pointing out that Pilate, Herod, and the people of Jerusalem all participated and shared in the guilt of crucifying Jesus. And as Peter stated when he preached the gospel after the Resurrection, "That is what has happened here in this city! For Herod Antipas, Pontius Pilate the governor, the Gentiles, and the people of Israel were all united against Jesus, your holy servant, whom you anointed" (Acts 4:27 NLT).

Pilate listened to the wrong voice and made the wrong decision. Tragically, he hardened his heart to the very voice of God. Herod didn't have the honor of hearing Jesus' voice, but Pilate did. Herod's heart was already hardened, but Pilate could that see Jesus was innocent. Deep down inside, he may have even thought Jesus was the Messiah. But then there was his career…his position…his power.

Judas sold his soul for thirty pieces of silver.

Herod traded his for an immoral lifestyle. And Pilate forfeited his for position, power, and prestige. What a story it could have been had he believed in Jesus on the spot. But history tells us that within seven years of this cruel deed, Pontius Pilate, the great Roman governor, was removed from high office by the governor of Syria. He was left broken, destitute, unwanted by Caesar, and all alone. Pilate threw his life away, because he was more concerned with what others thought about him than what God did. His craving for popularity and power cost him everything. And like Judas, he went out into the darkness of night and hung himself.

Better to succeed in God's eyes and fail in the world's.

We all know people like Pilate. Some of them choose their careers over Jesus. It is not that believers aren't allowed to have both, but they will pour themselves into the pursuit of success at the cost of everything else. They are willing to sacrifice their integrity, their standards, their friends, and even their faith for the results they can obtain. That is what Pilate did. And it's sad.

Others will choose people over Jesus. They are more concerned about what is cool or acceptable within their social group than what God wants or doesn't want. So they avoid standing up for what is right for fear of losing their social position. Pilate did that too. And it's tragic.

Better to succeed in God's eyes and fail in the world's. When Peter pointed out that he and the other disciples had left all they had to follow Jesus, the Lord replied, "No one who has left home or wife or brothers or parents or children for the sake of the kingdom of God will fail to receive many times as much in this age and, in the age to come, eternal life" (Luke 18:29–30).

Make your life's goal to please God, and just watch how He will bless you. Sure, you may lose some so-called friends here or a little social status there. But when it's all said and done, you will be glad that you chose to follow Him.

8 GOD'S MOST PAINFUL
MOMENT

John 19:25–30

C an you remember the most painful
moment of your life? There are different
types of pain, such as physical pain from a horrible
fall or a broken bone. It's an interesting thing
how the human body has a way of almost shutting
down temporarily in a state of shock so that you
actually don't feel the pain as severely. It is God's
protective system.

Then there are other kinds of pain that actually
can be worse than physical pain, such as the pain
of rejection, betrayal, or abandonment. It is the
kind of pain that comes from a husband saying,
"I've been unfaithful to you," or a wife saying,
"I want a divorce," or a child saying, "I don't
want to live the Christian life." It's the kind of
pain that comes when you are betrayed by a
friend, or perhaps by someone you did the
most for. It's the kind of pain cuts like a knife.

We are about to look at what I believe was the most painful moment in the earthly life and ministry of Jesus Christ. Of course, our minds immediately race to the act of the crucifixion itself, as the crude spikes were driven through His hands and feet. And that truly was horrific. We think of the cruel lashes on His back or the abuse He took from the soldiers. But as horrible as it was, that was not God's most painful moment. His worst moment of personal pain and anguish was humanity's greatest moment in its effect. In essence, His lowest moment was our highest. His pain was our gain.

His lowest moment was our highest.

At this point, Jesus had been through the horrific ordeals of scourging, beating, torture, and now, the crucifixion. In spite of all this, He gives seven statements.

SEVEN STATEMENTS

The first was, "Father, forgive them, for they do not know what they do" (Luke 23:34).

The second, made to one of the criminals being crucified with Him, was, "Assuredly, I say to you, today you will be with Me in Paradise" (Luke 23:43).

Now we come to His third statement:

> Now there stood by the cross of Jesus His mother, and His mother's sister, Mary the wife of Clopas, and Mary Magdalene. When Jesus therefore saw His mother, and the disciple whom He loved standing by, He said to His mother, "Woman, behold your son!" (vv. 25–26).

If I had been one of Jesus' followers on the day He was crucified, I wonder where I would have been found. After all, it is one thing to talk or sing about "coming to the cross," but it would have been quite a different thing altogether to do so on this dark day. The cross was a dangerous place to be. One would have needed a lot of courage to stand with Jesus that day, and at this point, most of His disciples were in hiding, one had betrayed Him, and another had denied Him. Only one of the Twelve stood with Him. A group of women, however, had the boldness to be there. Among them were His mother, Mary; Salome, who was the mother of James and John; and Mary Magdalene.

They were present out of devotion, not duty. They simply wanted to be with Jesus. So let's consider what the cross meant to these three women on the day that Jesus died.

A PLACE OF REDEMPTION

For Mary Magdalene, the cross was a place of redemption. Mary Magdalene had been under the power of demons when Jesus came and set her free. Her life was radically transformed that day, and she never was the same. On one occasion, when Jesus had been invited to dinner at the home of a Pharisee, an immoral woman came and anointed His feet with fragrant oil. Jesus told the disapproving Pharisees, "Therefore I say to you, her sins, which are many, are forgiven, for she loved much. But to whom little is forgiven, the same loves little" (Luke 7:47). Like this woman, Mary Magdalene had been forgiven of much. She wanted to be close to her Lord, even in death. She would be the first at His tomb on Easter Sunday as well. There at Calvary, she would rejoice in the redemption Jesus had given her.

A PLACE OF REBUKE

For Salome, the wife of Zebedee and the mother of James and John, the cross was a place of rebuke. We remember the brash request she brought before the Lord on behalf of her two sons, wanting to sit at His right and left when He established His kingdom. We can understand a mother's devotion, love, and ambition for her boys, but this was extreme. Jesus responded with a question to James and John, "Are you able to drink the cup that I drink, and be baptized with the baptism that I am baptized with?" (Mark 10:38).

His pain was our gain.

They both told Him, "We are able" (v. 39). But little did they—and their mother—realize the cup Jesus spoke of was the cross. Salome must have thought back on that conversation as she gazed sadly upon the beaten, bloodied, traumatized body of Jesus hanging there: *I wanted my sons to have places of honor at His right and left hand, but what I see there are crucified men.*

Thank God He doesn't answer all of our prayers (in the affirmative, at least). As James 4:3 explains, "When you ask, you do not receive, because you ask with wrong motives, that you may spend what you get on your pleasures" (NIV). Salome must have been ashamed and embarrassed, just as all of us eventually are when we pray selfishly.

A PLACE OF REWARD

For Mary, the mother of Jesus, the cross was a place of reward. It's interesting that we find Mary at the beginning of John's Gospel (John 2) and at the end (John 19), but nowhere in between. That isn't to say her role wasn't important, but it is not the focus in this or in any of the other three Gospels. Clearly she was the most blessed woman who ever lived, but we should not worship or pray to or through her to Jesus. Like any other sinner, Mary had to admit her sin and turn to Christ. In the Magnificat, Mary said, "My soul glorifies the Lord and my spirit rejoices in God *my Savior*" (Luke 1:46–47 NIV, emphasis mine). Having said that, what strength she showed on this day.

Imagine the anguish she must have felt at this moment. She had reared Him from childhood.

She knew His utter perfection better then anyone. Imagine being one of Jesus' siblings. I wonder if they were often told, "Why can't you be more like Jesus?" Or she may have literally said to them, "Now, what would Jesus do?" Yet, here she was, watching this wicked crowd of mockers hurl insults at her dear Son. His beaten, bloodied body was hanging on a Roman cross, and all she could do was watch. No loving mother ever wants to outlive her child, yet here was Jesus, dying in the prime of His life.

The once-tiny forehead she had kissed was now crowned with thorns.

The once-tiny forehead she had kissed was now crowned with thorns. The once-tiny hands and feet that she guided had been pierced and nailed to the cross. Those lips she had nursed were now parched and bloodied. And the once-tiny frame she had held in her arms was now being crucified. His disciples may have forsaken Him, but she was by His side until the end.

And she *stood* there. She would not give in to hysterics, running away in horror. She would not faint or crumple to the ground. She would be strong for Jesus and stand there. She was the very model of courage. She might have thought thirty years back to that day when she and Joseph (now deceased) had dedicated the child Jesus in the temple.

---

*Privilege brings responsibility
and sometimes pain.*

There was an old man named Simeon who said, "For my eyes have seen Your salvation which You have prepared before the face of all peoples, a light to bring revelation to the Gentiles, and the glory of Your people Israel" (Luke 2:32). Turning to Mary, he then said, "Behold, this Child is destined for the fall and rising of many in Israel, and for a sign which will be spoken against (yes, a sword will pierce through your own soul also), that the thoughts of many hearts may be revealed" (vv. 34–35).

The greatest privilege would bring with it the greatest of sorrows. Mary had faced difficulties from the very beginning when God touched her and Jesus was conceived in her womb. Her reputation was questioned. The Pharisees, at one point, told Jesus, "We were not born of fornication; we have one Father—God" (John 8:41). The scandalous implication was that Mary had conceived Jesus out of wedlock. At one point, she made the long, difficult journey to Bethlehem while she was far along in her pregnancy, and she gave birth to her firstborn in a stable. We love to romanticize the Christmas story, but the fact is that it was a long, hard journey and a terribly unsanitary place to give birth. The barn smelled of animals and urine, and the wind was cold. Then after Jesus was born, Mary and Joseph had to flee to Egypt, because Herod wanted to kill the baby Messiah. Many small children were killed in Bethlehem as the paranoid tyrant searched for the Child. Then there was that day when, after a frantic search, Mary and Joseph found Him in the temple. The young boy Jesus said, "Why did you seek Me? Did you not know that I must be about My Father's business?" (Luke 2:49).

At the cross as she took all this in, surely the sword pierced her own soul as the prophet Simeon said it would. This reminds us that privilege brings responsibility and sometimes pain. We sometimes wish we could do what certain spiritual leaders do.

But they have paid a price. And you don't know that until you have met them or have been them.

But something very profound was happening here to Mary. Perhaps as she looked up at Him, it all began to come into focus. Perhaps for the first time, she realized that Jesus was not her child, but she was His. Jesus, seeing her, then gave His third statement from the cross:

> When Jesus therefore saw His mother, and the disciple whom He loved standing by, He said to His mother, "Woman, behold your son!" Then He said to the disciple, "Behold your mother!" And from that hour that disciple took her to his own home. (vv. 26–27)

When Jesus said to Mary, "Behold your Son," I don't believe He was referring to himself, but to John.

A PLACE OF RESPONSIBILITY

For John, the cross was a place of responsibility. Remember, Jesus was reigning from the cross. He was completely in control of himself and the situation. That is one reason why He refused to drink the pain-numbing wine that was offered before He was crucified. He wanted to be in complete control of his faculties. He wanted to have His wits about Him. So when Jesus said to John, "Son, behold your mother," He was restoring John. Remember, John had joined the other disciples in forsaking Him and running away at the Garden of Gethsemane. But in John's defense, it was risky being there at the cross. Yet there stood, and he was forgiven and restored. You and I may stray from God's path. We may disobey God's will. We may even deny Him as Peter did. But we can always come back to the cross for forgiveness.

Jesus was concerned about people in this life, as well as preparing them for the next one.

Jesus not only restored John, but He honored him. It was as though Jesus were saying, "John, you're taking My place. Be a son to Mary and take care of her." But why not leave that responsibility to Mary's other children? Because John 7:5 tells us, "For even His brothers did not believe in Him." They became believers *after* the Resurrection, so there may even have been a rift in the family over this. Jesus was making provision for Mary.

We, too, have been called to take His place now that He's gone back to heaven. I don't mean that literally, of course, but we are His representatives. While He was here, Jesus said, "As long as I am in the world, I am the light of the world" (John 9:5). But now He says to us, "*You* are the light of the world. A city that is set on a hill cannot be hidden" (Matt. 5:14, emphasis mine).

You might have thought that Jesus would have given Mary some hint of the meaning of His mysterious suffering. Or He might have spoken to her of His Father's house that was waiting for those who trusted in Him. But at this moment, Jesus was more interested—as far as Mary was concerned—in the here and now, not the by and by. That is not to say the afterlife is not of the greatest importance, because it is. But Jesus was concerned about people in this life, as well as preparing them for the next one. Both are of the greatest importance to God. He not only offers us life after death, but life during life as well.

It is fascinating to see how much of the earthly ministry of Jesus was devoted to providing for the physical needs of people. He would heal their blindness, fill their stomachs, and calm their fears, as well as save their souls. And in the chapters to come, we'll see Him doing this even after His resurrection.

My friend, Franklin Graham, president of Samaritan's Purse, was sharing how in the aftermath of Hurricane Katrina, he had spoken with government officials who told him, "Before FEMA or the Red Cross or any government agency arrived, the church was here." Church vans came from around the nation, and believers were helping, bringing in food and water. Samaritan's Purse sent teams out to remove trees and repair roofs, and along with their help, they gave out Bibles. Not one person refused them.

Here on the cross, Jesus remembered that His mother must have a roof over her head and food to eat, and He charged John with that blessed responsibility.

THE DAY THE WORLD WENT DARK

And now came an ominous moment. It is here that the crucifixion reached its horrific climax in what has been described as "the crucifixion in the crucifixion." Without explanation, the sky turned dark. And from noon until 3:00 P.M., darkness fell across the land. The Greek word for "land" can be translated "Earth," indicating the world. This would not be the first time we read of in Scripture where God had done this. He caused a great darkness to cover the land of Egypt (see Ex. 10:21–22). And some forty years later, He caused the sun to stand still during one of Israel's battles (see Josh. 10:12–14).

Some extrabiblical sources also suggest that such a universal darkness occurred. A Roman historian mentioned it, and there supposedly was a report from Pilate to Emperor Tiberius that assumed the emperor's knowledge of a certain, widespread darkness, even mentioning that it took place from 12:00 to 3:00 in the afternoon. This darkness was probably a sign of God's judgment. Isaiah spoke of "darkness and distress" that would cover the land: "In that day they will roar against them like the roaring of the sea. And if one looks to the land, behold, darkness and sorrow; and the light is darkened by the clouds" (Isa. 5:30).

The Creator was dying on the cross, and all creation, shrouded in darkness, was sympathizing with Him. Isaac Watts had this in mind when he wrote these words of his hymn, "Alas! And Did

My Savior Bleed":

> Well might the sun in darkness hide
> And shut his glories in,
> When Christ, the great Redeemer, died
> For man the creature's sin.

UNIVERSALLY ABANDONED

The darkness was pierced by the voice of Jesus as He made His fourth statement from the cross: "My God, My God, why have You forsaken Me?" (Matt. 27:46; Mark 15:34). No fiction writer would have had his or her hero say words like these. They surprise us, disarm us, and cause us to wonder what He meant. We are looking at something that, in many ways, is impossible for us as human beings to fathom.

No man or woman has ever experienced such loneliness and isolation as Jesus did at this point. First, Judas betrayed Him, but His other disciples stood with Him—until Gethsemane. Then they, too, fled. But Simon Peter was still following, albeit at a distance. Then he, too, turned away from the Lord, openly denying Him. But there was still the Father, who was always there. Jesus had said, "And He who sent Me is with Me. *The Father has not left*

Me alone, for I always do those things that please Him" (John 8:29, emphasis mine); and "Indeed the hour is coming, yes, has now come, that you will be scattered, each to his own, and will leave Me alone. *And yet I am not alone, because the Father is with Me*" (John 16:32, emphasis mine). But at the cross, God the Father turned away His face. Why? Because God, in all His holiness, could not look at sin. He is so holy that the seraphim veil their faces before Him, so holy that His friend Abraham, standing before Him, said, "I am but dust and ashes" (see Gen. 18:27), so holy that when Job came into His presence, he said, "Therefore I despise myself and repent in dust and ashes" (Job 42:6 NIV). So holy is God that Habakkuk said of Him, "You are of purer eyes than to behold evil, and cannot look on wickedness … " (Hab. 1:13).

Jesus entered the darkness so that we might walk in the light.

So the holy Father had to turn away His face and pour His wrath upon His own Son. For Jesus, that was the greatest sacrifice He could have possiblly made. His greatest pain occurred at this moment. He felt forsaken of God, because this was the necessary consequence of sin. For someone to feel forsaken of God is the penalty that naturally and inevitably follows his or her separation from God because of sin. Yet Jesus was forsaken of God so we don't have to be. Jesus was forsaken of God for a time so that we might enjoy His presence forever. Jesus was forsaken of God so that we might be forgiven. Jesus entered the darkness so that we might walk in the light.

As Christ hung there, He was bearing the sins of the world. He was dying as a substitute for others. To Him was imputed the guilt of our sins, and He was suffering the punishment for those sins on our behalf. And the very essence of that punishment was the outpouring of God's wrath against sinners. The Father was pouring out the full measure of His wrath against sin, and the recipient of that wrath was God's own beloved Son. God was punishing Jesus as though He had personally committed every vile sin. In doing so, He could then treat those who believed in Him as if they had lived His perfect, righteous life.

Scripture clearly teaches this is what took place on the cross: "For He made Him who knew no sin to be sin for us, that we might become the righteousness of God in Him" (2 Cor. 5:21). And we read in Isaiah,

> Surely He has borne our griefs and carried our sorrows; yet we esteemed Him stricken, smitten by God, and afflicted. But He was wounded for our transgressions, He was bruised for our iniquities; the chastisement for our peace was upon Him, and by His stripes we are healed. (Isa. 53:5)

The physical pains of crucifixion, horrible as they were, were nothing when compared to the wrath of the Father being poured out upon His Son. This is what caused His sweat to become like drops of blood in Gethsemane. This is why He looked ahead to the cross with such horror. We cannot even begin to fathom what He was going through at this time. All of our worst fears about the horrors of hell—and more—were realized by Him as He received the full impact of our sin. Never for one moment during His entire earthly life did He ever step outside of intimate fellowship with His Father. He was as spiritually sensitive and in tune with the Father as one could be. That is why this was for Jesus a fate worse than death. To be forsaken by the Father was the most difficult thing He had to bear.

―――⋙◈◈◈⋘―――

*To be forsaken by the Father was the
most difficult thing He had to bear.*

―――⋙◈◈◈⋘―――

This indeed was God's most painful moment.
This was the greatest sacrifice He could have
possibly made on our behalf.

This brings us back to the question that Jesus
asked (and we do, too, sometimes): "Why have You
forsaken Me?" Note that it was not a cry *against*
the Father, but *to* Him.

Many people in times of crisis will cry out *at*
God. They are angry with Him and accusing of
Him. "I'm mad at God!" they say. Or they doubt
God's wisdom in their circumstances. But this
wasn't the case with Jesus. His cry was, "My
God, and *My* God."

Job, after his suffering, said, "Though He slay
me, yet will I trust Him" (Job 13:15). And when
many of Jesus' followers were turning away, Peter
said, "Lord, to whom shall we go? You have the
words of eternal life" (John 6:68 NIV). When we
don't understand what God is doing, we should
always fall back on that which we do understand:
that He loves us and has our best interests in mind.

God has never forsaken anyone but His Son. You may have felt abandoned by God, but God has never forsaken you. Perhaps you feel alone, even forsaken, right now. Maybe it seems as though God has somehow forgotten you. But nothing could be further from the truth. Jesus was forsaken that we might never be forsaken. He experienced terrible loneliness and isolation so that we would never be alone. He was misunderstood so that we might know the truth and be set free. He died so that we might live. He has promised, "I will never leave you nor forsake you" (Heb. 13:5), and has said, "And lo, I am with you always, even to the end of the age" (Matt. 28:20).

A SYMPATHETIC HIGH PRIEST

Now came the fifth statement from the cross, and the first of a personal nature:

> After this, Jesus, knowing that all things were now accomplished, that the Scripture might be fulfilled, said, "I thirst!" Now a vessel full of sour wine was sitting there; and they filled a sponge with sour wine, put it on hyssop, and put it to His mouth. (vv. 28–29)

Up to this point, Jesus had been focusing only on the needs of others. He had been concerned with those who crucified Him, with the criminal who called upon Him, and with the mother who bore Him, and finally, the sins of the whole world. He had been so busy thinking of others that He hadn't thought of himself.

Many of those who are suffering today would forget much of their personal pain if they focused on the needs of others. That is not to say that we don't have personal battles to fight or struggles to deal with. But if you think your life is hard living in the United States, then you need to visit a developing nation. Or if you are discouraged about your aches and pains, then you need to visit a person with cancer. It puts things into perspective.

Jesus was forsaken that we might never be forsaken.

This thirst Jesus was experiencing was burning and severe. Scientists tell us that thirst is the most agonizing of all pain. Every cell in the body cries out for relief, and the pain only gets worse and worse as time goes by. This shows Jesus' humanity, and that He practiced what He prayed. He has already prayed, "Father forgive them. …" Now, He asks for water—from His enemies no less. Some of us do not like to ask favors of anyone. But on those occasions when we do ask for a favor, we ask it of a very close friend. Jesus was so forgiving that He was willing to ask a favor from an enemy. And it wasn't the first time He had asked for a drink of water from someone who wasn't very friendly. To the immoral Samaritan woman, He said, "Please give me a drink."

She looked at Him with hard eyes and asked, "Why would you, a Jew, ask me for a drink?"

Jesus told her, "If you knew the gift of God, you would ask, and I would give you living water."

Here, Jesus was asking for some water, and a brave soldier gave it to Him. We don't know this man's name, but Jesus did. He could literally say of this man, "I was thirsty, and you gave Me water." But we can still do this for Jesus today. Remember, He said, " 'For I was hungry and you gave Me food; I was thirsty and you gave Me drink; I was a stranger and you took Me in; I was naked and you clothed Me; I was sick and you visited Me; I was in prison and you came to Me…inasmuch as you did it to one of the least of these My brethren, you did it to Me' " (Matt. 25:35–36, 40).

We make much about the deity of Jesus, of the fact that He was "God with us"—and so we should. But that fact that He said, "I thirst," shows us His very real humanity. As Hebrews tells us, "For we do not have a High Priest who cannot sympathize with our weaknesses, but was in all points tempted as we are, yet without sin" (Heb. 4:15). He was called "a man of sorrows," so no matter how great your need or difficulty, you can know He understands. You can "cast all your anxiety on him because he cares for you" (1 Pet. 5:7 NIV). Jesus Christ is able to sympathize and identify with us in our pains and needs, so we can come boldly to the throne of grace.

WHAT DOES IT MEAN TO YOU?

What is the cross for you today? Is it a place of redemption as it was for Mary Magdalene? Is it a place where you are reminded of your need for a Savior, a place where you see the blackness of your sin in contrast to its blazing light? Then call on Him today.

Or, is it a place of rebuke, as it was for Salome? Is it a place where you realize there is sin in your life that needs to be dealt with? Is there selfishness in your prayers, unkindness in your actions, or pride in your heart? Then turn from that sin.

Is it a place of reward, as it was for Mary? Is it a place where you stand in awe as you realize all Christ has purchased for you, having removed your sin and placed His righteousness into your account? Then rejoice in that.

Perhaps, for you, it is a place of responsibility as it was for John. It is a place where you are reminded there are strangers to feed and lost people to reach? If so, then do those things.

THE BATTLE CRY OF THE CROSS

Now Jesus would finish what He had begun, which brings us to the sixth of His seven statements from the cross: "When he had received the drink, Jesus said, 'It is finished.' With that, he bowed his head and gave up his spirit" (v. 30 NIV). This sixth statement from the cross was not the whimper of a defeated man. It was the triumphant shout of victory of the Son of God. At the age of 33, most people are saying "It is beginning!" But at the age of 33, Jesus was saying, "It is finished!"

*No matter how great your need or
difficulty, you can know He understands.*

He didn't say "I am finished." His wasn't the
shout of a victim overwhelmed by circumstances.
His was the shout of a victor who had overcome
all His enemies. In Greek, the statement is one
word, consisting of ten letters: *tetelestai*.
It means, "It is finished, it *stands* finished, and
it *always will* be finished."

Another Gospel tells us He shouted this with a
loud voice. I call it the battle cry of the cross. It's as
if to say, "The war is over!" These words were not
only heard in the ears of those who stood close by
at the foot of the cross: the soldiers, the group of
brave women, and John. They also reverberated, no
doubt, through the forces of heaven and hell. In the
presence of the Father, they were a cry of victory,
as a new covenant and relationship with God and
humankind was now made available.

And these words most likely reverberated
through the hallways of hell and its forces as well,
as it was realized what a horrendous mistake the
crucifixion was for their cause. In a blind rage of

hatred and jealousy, Satan filled the heart of Judas Iscariot to betray and help in the crucifixion of Jesus Christ. But what he unwittingly did was play into the plan and purpose of the Father, who had determined long before there was a solar system, or a planet called Earth, or a Garden called Eden, that God would come here and atone for the sins of the world.

<hr />

If ever you are tempted to doubt God's love for you, look at the cross.

<hr />

"It is finished!" or "*Tetelestai*!" was a commonplace term in the first century. It was used by workers when they had completed a job: "Tetelesai— I have finished the work you gave me to do." This meant they had done the job their master had given to them. Jesus Christ had completed the job the Father had given Him to do. As we read earlier, Jesus prayed, "I have finished the work which You have given Me to do" (John 17:4). One day, we all will have to give an account of what we have done with our lives. Romans 14:12 says, "So then, each of us will give an account of himself to God" (NIV). We need to find the work God has given us to do…and then do it.

Tetelestai was also a term used by artists when they completed a task. When an artists had finished his work, he would step back and say, "Tetelestai!— the picture is completed!"

Other ways this word *tetelestai* is translated are, "It is made an end of"; "It is paid"; "It is performed"; and "It is accomplished." What was made an end of? It was our sins and the guilt that accompanied them.

What was paid? It was the price of our redemption.

What was performed? It was the righteous requirements of the law.

What was accomplished? The work the Father had given Him to do.

All of the Old Testament sacrifices were pointing to what Jesus would do on the cross. John the Baptist said of Him, "Behold! The Lamb of God who takes away the sin of the world!" (John 1:29). It was hard for His followers when He was crucified. They probably felt like *they* were finished. All their hopes and dreams were dashed as they looked at their dead leader hanging on that cross. But everything was proceeding as God had planned it.

When Jesus joined the two disciples on the Emmaus Road, He corrected them, taking them to the Old Testament passages that pointed to Him: "O foolish ones, and slow of heart to believe in all that the prophets have spoken!" (Luke 24:25).

The storm had finally passed, the cup He had been given had been drained, the devil had done his worst, and the Lord had bruised him. The darkness had ended.

Sin is not small, because it is not against a small God.

Three times on the cross, Jesus had addressed God: "Father forgive them . . ." (His first statement); "My God, My God . . ." (His fourth statement); and now, His seventh and final statement: "Father, 'into Your hands I commit My spirit' " (Luke 23:46). Jesus had addressed the Father at the beginning, the middle, and the end. And we should do the same in life. One day, we will breathe our last breath and leave this world. May we be calling on our Father as well. Often in our youth, we will think of God. But then we will stray and throw away years of our lives. How glorious it is to know and serve the Lord at the beginning, middle, and end of your life.

As we have looked at what Jesus went through leading up to, and on, the cross, we may wonder, "But *why* did He have to suffer and die like this?"

He suffered and died to show His love for us. Jesus said, "For God so loved the world that He gave His only begotten Son, that whoever believes in Him should not perish but have everlasting life" (John 3:16). And Ephesians 5:25 tells us, "Christ also loved the church and gave Himself for her." The apostle Paul said, "I live by faith in the Son of God, who loved me and gave Himself for me" (Gal. 2:20). So if ever you are tempted to doubt God's love for you, look at the cross.

He also suffered and died to absorb the wrath of God. If God were not just, there would be no demand for His Son to suffer and die. And if God were not loving, there would be no willingness for His Son to suffer and die. But God is both just and loving. At the cross, God lovingly met His own demands for justice. God says in His Word, "The soul who sins shall die" (Ez. 18:4, 20), and "All have sinned and fall short of the glory of God" (Romans 3:23). So you see, sin is not small, because it is not against a small God. The seriousness of an insult rises with the dignity of the one insulted. We have sinned against and have offended God. So that just and loving God sent Jesus as the substitute for us. God's wrath that should have been placed on us was placed on Him.

In addition, He suffered and died to cancel the legal demands against us. Conventional wisdom says that God "grades on the curve." In other words, if our good deeds outweigh our bad deeds, then we are okay. But that is neither biblical nor true. If we are saved from the consequences of our bad deeds, it will not be because they weighed less than our good deeds. Salvation isn't attained by balancing records. It is only acquired by canceling records! This is why Jesus suffered and died for us. Colossians 2:13–14 says, "He forgave all our sins. He canceled the record that contained the charges against us. He took it and destroyed it by nailing it to Christ's cross" (NLT).

Finally, Jesus suffered and died to provide our forgiveness and justification. "Since we have now been justified by his blood, how much more shall we be saved from God's wrath through him!" (Rom. 5:9 NIV). To be justified means to be forgiven of the wrong we have done. But it is also a legal term that means, "Just as if it never happened." He forgave you of your debt and then put the riches of Christ into your account. This is not something that happens over a period of time because you've earned it. Rather, it's something that is instantaneously allotted to every person who has put his or her faith in Christ, no matter what he or she has done. It is not gradual; it's immediate.

Imagine being in debt for $10 million. You had charged yourself into oblivion, and there was no conceivable way to pay back those debts. In fact, you have exactly $1.34 in your checking account. Now, imagine that a complete stranger heard about your situation and said, "I love you so much, I am going to pay off your debts." And then he pays off your debt of $10 million.

You would say, "Thank you so much! I can't believe I'm debt-free!"

Then he says, "I think you ought to go down and check your account balance. So you go down to your local ATM machine, put in your card and your PIN, and check your account balance. You have a balance of $20 million! Not only did he forgive you of a debt of $10 million and pay it for you, but he put $20 million into your account!

Think about that for a moment. And then think about the fact that what God did for you is infinitely greater. Not only did God acquit you of your sins, but He allotted to your account the righteousness of Jesus Christ.

Now that's a lot to be thankful for. And it came as a result of God's most painful moment.

9 A NEW BEGINNING

John 20:1–18

Have you ever misunderstood what someone was saying? American corporations trying to break into international markets sometimes have had a very difficult time communicating uniquely American ideas and colloquialisms. The problem is that something often gets lost in the translation. In Italy, for example, a campaign for Schweppes Tonic Water translated the name into Schweppes Toilet Water.

When Coca-Cola was introduced in China, it was first rendered as "Ke-kou-ke-la." Unfortunately, the company did not discover until after thousands of signs had been printed that the phrase actually means, "Bite the wax tadpole," or "Female horse stuffed with wax," depending on the dialect.

Also in China, the Kentucky Fried Chicken slogan, "Finger-lickin' good," came out as, "Eat your fingers off."

In Taiwan, the translation of the Pepsi slogan, "Come alive with the Pepsi Generation," translated, "Pepsi will bring your ancestors back from the dead."

When General Motors introduced the Chevy Nova in South America, the company apparently was unaware that in Spanish, "*No va*" means, "It won't go."

THINGS AREN'T ALWAYS WHAT THEY SEEM

In the same way, when Jesus spoke to His disciples about His impending death and resurrection, it seemed to go right over their heads. They just didn't seem to get it; they weren't paying attention. Jesus spoke in plain and simple terms, yet it did not penetrate their minds and hearts. As they read the Old Testament, they saw the glory, but not the suffering. They saw the crown, but not the cross.

They saw the crown, but not the cross.

In their minds, Jesus had let them down. Of course He hadn't. But they thought He had. And for many, perception is often reality. Perhaps you feel that way today as well. Perhaps you feel as though God has somehow let you down, that He hasn't kept His promises. It wasn't that Jesus had failed, but they had failed to see what He had come to do. The same is true of us when it seems as though God has failed us. Perhaps we need a new understanding of His ways.

All the disciples could see was that their Master had been killed—and not just killed, but tortured, humiliated, and murdered in cold blood before their very eyes. When He uttered those words, "It is finished!" from Calvary, that was the end in their minds. It seemed for them that indeed it was finished.

Two disciples on the road to Emmaus pretty much summed up how everyone felt: "But we had hoped that he was the one who was going to redeem Israel" (Luke 24:21 NIV). Prior to the crucifixion, everything seemed to be progressing beautifully. When Jesus rode into Jerusalem, it appeared to the disciples that He was finally ready and willing to establish the kingdom as Israel's long-awaited Messiah. The people finally were discovering what the disciples knew all along: that Jesus of Nazareth was the long-awaited Messiah of Israel.

But then, without warning, everything began to unravel in the upper room. He just didn't sound like himself, speaking as though it were an end to something. Peter was so shocked to hear Jesus say that all of them would forsake Him, that he just had to separate himself from the rabble and protest, "Even if all fall away on account of you, I never will" (Matt. 26:33 NIV). But there in the Garden of Gethsemane, Peter was unnerved to see Jesus as he did. The Lord was weeping with His face to the ground. He was sweating and in obvious agony. Peter wanted to do something, and Jesus came to him and asked him to pray. But as the night wore on, Peter, with James and John, fell asleep from sorrow.

If the resurrection of Jesus is true, then it means there is life after death.

When the soldiers emerged on the scene, Peter felt that something needed to be done. But as they took the Lord away, he followed at a distance. His short-lived courage quickly gave way to fear. Then came that terrible incident when he did just what Jesus said he would do. He denied

Him. It was obvious that Jesus knew him better than he knew himself. His eyes looked into the eyes of Christ for a moment that seemed like an eternity, and then Jesus was whisked away and tried. The last sight he had of his Lord was as He hung on a cross, so beaten and bloodied that He was hardly recognizable.

Peter's entire life came crumbling down around him as all he had held dear in life now lay dead in a Roman tomb. He had so many regrets, and he never even had the opportunity to say he was sorry.

WHAT THE RESURRECTION MEANS

But what a difference a day makes! Jesus was to rise from the dead as He had promised repeatedly. This would forever change Peter—and a group of disillusioned, discouraged, and frightened followers—into bold and courageous disciples who turned their world upside-down.

Of course, not everyone believes Jesus Christ rose from the dead, and I think there are reasons for that. I don't think people reject Christ's resurrection because they have carefully researched it and have concluded that the evidence for its historicity and reality came up wanting. I think they reject it for the same reason they reject the biblical account of the Creation: If God did indeed create the world, then it means that we are not just highly evolved animals. It means we are responsible to our Creator and will have to answer for our actions. And if the resurrection of Jesus is true, then it means there *is* life after death.

The Bible teaches the real reason a person doesn't believe is not intellectual and rational, but moral and spiritual. David wrote, "The fool says in his heart, 'There is no God.' " (Ps. 14:1). The fact that the foolishness referred to is moral, and not intellectual, is clear from the rest of the text: "They are corrupt, their deeds are vile; there is no one who does good." Atheism's rejection of God appeals to people who wish to avoid judgment for their sinful lifestyles.

If you don't have God at the beginning, then you don't have God at the end. And you don't have God in the middle, either. If you believe that you evolved, then you say your life is an accident, maybe even a mistake. You have come from nowhere, you are going nowhere, and your life has no eternal purpose. You don't belong to anyone, and you have no accounting to give to anyone.

But we were created by God, and we will be judged by God: "For he has set a day when he will judge the world with justice by the man he has appointed. He has given proof of this to all men by raising him from the dead" (Acts 17:31 NIV). This reminds us, among other things, that God's justice ultimately will prevail. We have all witnessed wrongs committed against others (and ourselves). But it is all going to be settled at the judgment seat.

JESUS' FATAL TORMENT

Now let's briefly review what had happened to Jesus up to this point. In Gethsemane, His sweat became like drops of blood. We learned that this may have been a medical condition called hematidrosis, which occurs when tiny capillaries in the sweat glands rupture, mixing sweat with blood. As a result, the skin becomes extremely fragile. Jesus was then taken, beaten repeatedly, and flogged thirty-nine times with a whip replete with razor-sharp bones and lead balls, reducing His body to quivering ribbons of bleeding flesh.

As Jesus slumped in a pool of His own blood, the soldiers threw a scarlet robe across His shoulders and pressed a crown of thorns into His scalp. Then they took the "scepter" out of His hand and beat him with it. Jesus, who would have been in critical condition by this time, had a three-hundred-pound cross placed on His shoulder as He made His way through the city. He then was laid on it, as seven-inch iron spikes were driven through His hands and feet. Waves of pain pulsated through Christ's body as the nails lacerated His nerves.

Breathing was agonizing as Jesus hung on the cross. The sin of the entire world was placed upon Him as He cried, *"Eli, Eli, lama sabachthani? … My God, My God, why have You forsaken Me?"* Jesus then died.

We were created by God, and we will be judged by God.

To prove He was indeed dead, a Roman legionnaire drove his spear through Jesus' side. Blood and water rushed from the wound, demonstrating that Jesus had suffered fatal torment: "But one of the soldiers pierced His side with a spear, and immediately blood and water came out" (John 19:34). John, living in the first century, most likely would not have known what twenty-first century medical science has only recently discovered: blood and water flowed from the side of Jesus, due to the fact that the hearts is surrounded by a sack of water called a pericardium. The water came from the pierced pericardium of Christ, and the blood came from His pierced heart. As one expert said, "Even if Jesus were alive before He was stabbed, the lance would have almost certainly killed Him!"

The Roman guards actually were the first to report His death. They were experts at execution and would be put to death themselves if they allowed a condemned man to escape death. In fact, they were so certain He was dead that they didn't even bother to break His legs.

THE DAY THAT CHANGED EVERYTHING

Now let's go back in time to the day that changed everything. We will see specifically how the resurrection of Jesus affected three people: Mary, Peter, and John:

> Now on the first day of the week Mary Magdalene went to the tomb early, while it was still dark, and saw that the stone had been taken away from the tomb. Then she ran and came to Simon Peter, and to the

other disciple, whom Jesus loved, and said to them, "They have taken away the Lord out of the tomb, and we do not know where they have laid Him." (vv. 1–2)

Luke 8:2 simply describes Mary Magdalene as someone "out of whom had come seven demons." Imagine that for moment. She most likely had lived a very wicked life. She would have been an evil and tormented person. New Testament accounts of demon possession record the manifestations of self-inflicted wounds, violence, and mental disorders, among other things. Mary had been completely under the control of evil—until Jesus that is.

It's doubtful that anyone believed in His power more than Mary.

From that moment on, she completely turned her back on her previous life. And she became a fervent, devoted follower of Christ. From then on, whenever the Gospels list the names of the female followers of Jesus, Mary's name is always listed first. She joined a group of women who helped support Jesus and His disciples, and she became one of His most enthusiastic supporters.

It's doubtful that anyone believed in His power more than Mary. No one watched Him more closely, no one loved Him more deeply, and no one gave to Him more freely. She had followed Jesus from Galilee to care for His needs and provided whatever she could from her savings. What was mere money, after all, when He had restored her life?

But now He was dead and buried.

She probably had a sleepless night and could not wait until the break of day. So early the next morning, Mary rose and was joined by another Mary, the wife of Clopas; Salome, and others. All they wanted to do was to anoint his dead body. They knew they couldn't bring Him back. It was the first-century equivalent of wanting to place a beautiful bouquet of flowers on someone's grave. You just want to do something—anything. As they made their way to the tomb, they were concerned about how to move the stone so they could get in. They arrived at the tomb and were shocked to find the stone had been rolled away. I don't think it even crossed Mary's or the other women's minds that Jesus had risen. They thought someone had taken the body. But why? Who? And where?

The ladies huddled and decided that Peter and John should be told. Mary was either dispatched or she volunteered, and then she made her way to where they were.

Meanwhile, the other women cautiously approached the empty tomb. There they saw angels:

> But the angel answered and said to the women, "Do not be afraid, for I know that you seek Jesus who was crucified. He is not here; for He is risen, as He said. Come, see the place where the Lord lay. And go quickly and tell His disciples that He is risen from the dead, and indeed He is going before you into Galilee; there you will see Him. Behold, I have told you." So they went out quickly from the tomb with fear and great joy, and ran to bring His disciples word. (Matt. 28:5–8)

Meanwhile, Mary found Peter and John, and they both ran back to the tomb, leaving Mary in their dust:

> Both were running, but the other disciple outran Peter and reached the tomb first. He bent over and looked in at the strips of linen lying there but did not go in. Then Simon Peter, who was behind him, arrived and went into the tomb. He saw the strips of

linen lying there, as well as the burial cloth that had been around Jesus' head. The cloth was folded up by itself, separate from the linen. Finally the other disciple, who had reached the tomb first, also went inside. He saw and believed. (vv. 4–8 NIV)

Notice from verse 4 that John outran Peter. Why do we have this little detail? Was it because John was the "other disciple" mentioned in this verse, and he just wanted us to know that he won? I think there may be a spiritual reason as well.

THREE PEOPLE, THREE REACTIONS

When you were a little child and had disobeyed, if your mother said to you, "Just wait until your Father gets home, … " would you run to meet him as you normally would when his car pulled into the driveway? Not with a guilty conscience.

The first human preacher of the Resurrection was a woman.

Remember, Peter's last contact with Jesus was when he had denied Him in the firelight of Caiaphas' courtyard. Yes, Peter was running to the tomb, but he probably had mixed emotions, to say the least. And this would also explain the way he looked into the tomb.

Here in the text, we find three different reactions to the empty tomb, that of Mary, Peter, and John. John tells us that Mary "looked into the tomb" (v. 11), Peter "saw" (v. 6), and John "saw and believed" (v. 8).

The word used to describe the way Mary looked into the empty tomb simply means she saw—just the ordinary word. The word used to describe Peter's looking is quite different. It means, "He looked carefully and critically." He was not sure what to make of it. Luke's Gospel tells us he went home again, "marveling to himself at what had happened" (Luke 24:12).

God can do extraordinary things through ordinary people.

Lastly, we see John's reaction. The word used for his looking into the tomb means, "He perceived and understood." John, the "apostle of love," always seemed to have a unique spiritual perception. At the Sea of Galilee, when a stranger called from shore, "Boys, do you have any fish?" it was John who immediately knew who it was and said, "It's the Lord!" Apparently, all that time leaning on Jesus' chest seemed to help.

It's interesting how several people can see the same thing in different ways. We see this in Peter, John, and Mary, as well as with men and women in general.

For example, when a husband and wife are out driving and he loses his way, she says, "Let's ask for directions."

But he hears, "You're not a man."

She says, "Can I have the remote control?"

He hears, "Let's watch something that will bore us beyond belief!"

She says, "I would like to redecorate."

He hears, "Let's take our money and flush it down the toilet."

She says, "You need to get in touch with your feelings."

He hears, "Blah, blah, blah."

She says, "Are you listening to me?"

He hears, "Blah, blah, blah."

It all depends on how you look at things.

ALONE AT THE TOMB

So now, everyone is gone, except Mary. She is alone, totally deserted. And she is still wondering where the body of Jesus is. She is at the breaking point and simply bursts out in tears. There are angels in the tomb, and they ask her why she is weeping.

Mary's persistent faith and love was richly rewarded.

"Because they have taken away my Lord, and I do not know where they have laid Him," she tells them. Mary didn't care much about angels. They may have impressed the other women, who bowed before them, but not Mary. All she wanted was Jesus. When she watched Him die, she was lost. Now, she has only her own pain, and her heart has once again become as empty as the tomb—and just as desolate. Not knowing where to go, she just stood there alone.

Maybe she thought to herself, *What do I do now? I can't go back to what I used to do. I have wealth, but for what purpose? Financial freedom isn't enough freedom without some meaning.* If the song, "I'd Rather Have Jesus," had been written by this time, Mary could have sung it:

> I'd rather have Jesus than silver or gold,
> I'd rather be His than have riches untold;
> I'd rather have Jesus than houses or lands,
> I'd rather be led by His nail pierced hand.
> Than to be the king of a vast domain
> And be held in sin's dread sway;
> I'd rather have Jesus than anything
> This world affords today.[1]

Then a voice spoke, "Woman, why are you weeping? Whom are you seeking? Thinking He was the gardener, she said, "Sir, if You have carried Him away, tell me where You have laid Him, and I will take Him away" (v. 15). She was willing to carry the full weight of the body of Jesus, plus the 100-pound weight of the anointing spices. Even if Jesus were slight of weight, Mary was offering—without thinking—to carry the weight that would be more than a strong man could carry. But she didn't think of this, because she loved the Lord. How touched Jesus must have been by this statement.

Softly and tenderly, Jesus said, "Mary."

Suddenly, like a bolt of lightning, Mary

recognized this voice. It was Jesus!

"Rabboni!" she cried out, which means "Master," or "Teacher." Then she flew to Jesus and wrapped her arms around Him, like a drowning person clutching her rescuer.

Jesus then said, "Do not cling to Me for I have not yet ascended to My Father; but go to My brethren and say to them, 'I am ascending to My Father and your Father, and to My God and your God" (v. 17).

That which had been the worst defeat was now the greatest of all victories.

What did this mean? After all, a few verses later, He invited Thomas to touch Him. And in Matthew's Gospel, we read, "So they came and held Him by the feet and worshiped Him" (Matt. 28:9). His words presented an entirely new command, because never before had He told anyone to stay away from Him. His words to Mary could be translated, "Stop clinging to Me." It was as if to say, "Don't cling to me in the old way. Things are different now. This sobbing, wanting to hold onto the physical must change. In the past, I was there for you to reach out and touch. But things are going to change now. They will be even better, because I am going to live in your heart! You never will be separated from Me again. So don't cling to me in that old way."

Note also his reference to the Father: "My Father and your Father." Throughout the Old Testament, "God" had been the name by which Israel thought of the Almighty. The term, "Father," had remained almost unknown. When the Lord taught His disciples to pray "Our Father, … " this had been something new to them. It was a New Covenant, a new relationship. No longer would they have to go through the High Priest once a year. Now Jesus would be available twenty-four hours a day.

Mary couldn't wait to tell the others: "Mary Magdalene came and told the disciples that she had seen the Lord, and that He had spoken these things to her" (v. 18). It's interesting whom the Lord chose to appear to first: a woman. The first human preacher of the Resurrection was a woman. She rushed to tell the men, who immediately doubted. It's hard for us to appreciate how significant this was. Among the Jews in that day, the testimony of a woman wasn't held in high regard. The Rabbis taught, "It is better that the words of the Law be burned than be delivered to a woman."

By appearing first to Mary, Jesus was essentially saying, "Oh, yeah? Well check this out, boys! I am choosing a woman to be the first to proclaim my message!"

FOUR LESSONS FROM THE RESURRECTION

There are many applications for us from this story, reminders for our lives, if you will.

First, the Resurrection reminds us that God loves ordinary, and especially flawed, people. They didn't come any more ordinary or flawed than Peter, John, and Mary. Remember, Mary once was a wicked woman, but Jesus transformed her life. He not only forgave her, but He called her along with Peter, John, and others to be His messengers and representatives. This brings hope to all who were the last picked for the team, the ones who did not break records, win contests, or distinguish themselves from the crowd. But God can do extraordinary things through ordinary people.

Second, the Resurrection reminds us that God blesses those who seek Him with all their heart.

There is no question that Mary's persistent faith and love was richly rewarded. She was the last at the cross and the first at the tomb. She cared little for the social ramifications, whether it was popular, or even if it meant her life. She loved Jesus, and she wanted the world to know. She made time early in the morning and found the risen Lord. Do you make time for Jesus in your schedule? We are all busy. But we always seem to find time for what is important to us. God said, "And you will seek Me and find Me, when you search for Me with all your heart" (Jer. 29:13).

Death is not the end.

Third, the Resurrection reminds us that God will more than meet us halfway. Mary was weak in her faith, but strong in her love for Jesus. She came with what she had, and Jesus met her more than halfway. Perhaps your faith has been weakened. Maybe tragedy has befallen you, a loved one has died, or a marriage has collapsed. Your faith and hope have suffered. Jesus is calling your name, just as He called Mary's.

Finally, the Resurrection gives us hope for now and eternity. Mary was so excited, because that which had been the worst defeat was now the greatest of all victories.

It reminds me of a story I heard about the Battle of Waterloo. It was June 18, 1815, and the French, under the command of Napoleon, were fighting the allied forces of the British, Dutch, and Germans under the command of Wellington. The people of England depended on a system of signals to find out how the battle was going. One of these signals was on the tower of Winchester Cathedral. Late in the day, it flashed the message: "W-E-L-L-I-N-G-T-O-N---D-E-F-E-A-T-E-D---" At that moment, a cloud of fog made it impossible to read the message. The news of defeat quickly spread throughout the city. The people were devastated when they heard their country had lost the war. Suddenly, the fog lifted, and the remainder of the message could be read. It was discovered the message had four words, not two. The complete message said, "W-E-L-L-I-N-G-T-O-N---D-E-F-E-A-T-E-D---T-H-E---E-N-E-M-Y!" It took only a few minutes for the good news to spread. Sorrow was turned into joy, defeat was turned into victory!

The same happened at the resurrection of Jesus. Hope had died in the hearts of His disciples. After the crucifixion, the fog of disappointment and misunderstanding had crept in on the friends of Jesus. They had read only part of the message: "Christ defeated. ..." But then on the third day, the fog of disappointment and misunderstanding lifted, and the world received the complete message.

This is really the great message of the resurrection of Jesus: Death is not the end. As 1 Thessalonians 4:14 tells us, "For if we believe that Jesus died and rose again, even so God will bring with Him those who sleep in Jesus." And in 1 Corinthians we read, "But now Christ is risen from the dead, and has become the firstfruits of those who have fallen asleep. For since by man came death, by Man also came the resurrection of the dead. For as in Adam all die, even so in Christ all shall be made alive" (1 Cor. 15:20–22).

Because Jesus both died and rose again, we shall be raised like Him. Now that's what I call a new beginning.

10   JESUS AND THE
SKEPTIC

John 20:19–31

All my life, I have always asked lots of questions. It is because of my upbringing, which, in many ways, was really no upbringing at all, due to my mom's alcoholic lifestyle.

I was passed off from living with her, to my grandparents, to aunts, to military school, and then back to my mom again. I learned to be self-sufficient and had to develop survival skills to… well, survive. As a result, peer pressure didn't impact me as strongly as it did others. I learned to think for myself. I also learned it was hard to trust people, because many that I had trusted let me down. Yet I always longed for something pure, true, and good. I would lose myself in movies with happy endings. All this was because I had to face the reality of the life I was actually living.

So when I first encountered Christians, it was hard for me to wrap my mind around the concept. I thought this was something you only found in movies. I thought, *Jesus can't do all the things these Christians say He can.* I was skeptical and doubtful it could happen to someone like me. But at the same time, my desire for something good and right drove me on. So, I took that leap of faith and gave my heart to Jesus Christ.

Some Christians are reluctant to admit they have any questions at all.

After my conversion, I had my share of doubts. *Was this real? Was God going to really work in my life? Could God ever have a plan for someone like me? Could I ever actually live this Christian life?*

DARING TO DOUBT

Have you ever had doubts like these? Many of us, even deeply committed believers, would have to admit that we struggle with doubt now and then. Some Christians are reluctant to admit they have any questions at all. I think sometimes we have the idea that to question God is an act of spiritual treason or betrayal, or that doubt is an unpardonable sin. But I am confident that if we were honest, we could all admit to having struggled with doubt at times.

Has it ever seemed like God has let you down? Has something ever happened in your life that caused you to say, "Where is God?" or "What exactly is God doing?" Have you ever needed an answer from God and wondered why He was silent? He could have spoken one word and solved your problem; He could have done *something* to resolve your situation. Yet it seemed as though He was holding back, oblivious to your needs, or not really paying attention. In times like these, it might seem like entertaining doubt is clearly wrong and indicates a lack of faith. But Oswald Chambers said, "Doubt is not always a sign that a man is wrong. It may be a sign that he is thinking." You see, God loves skeptics too. In fact, it's been said that "skepticism is the first step toward truth." And though God loves skeptics, He wants to turn them into believers.

You may be surprised to know that some of God's greatest servants had times of doubt and uncertainty. Moses was ready to quit on at least one occasion. After listening to the complaints of Israel, he said, "I am not able to bear all these people alone, because the burden is too heavy for me. If You treat me like this, please kill me here and now—if I have found favor in Your sight—and do not let me see my wretchedness!" (Numbers 11:14–15). To me, that sounds like a pretty discouraged guy who was having his share of doubts.

The great prophet, Elijah, too, was ready to throw in the towel. After the showdown on Mount Carmel and hearing of Jezebel's threats, he became discouraged, uncertain, and doubtful. Like Moses, he wanted it all to be over. He said to God, "It is enough! Now Lord, take my life, for I am no better than my fathers!" (1 Kings 19:4).

God loves skeptics too.

The apostle Paul was discouraged as well. He wrote to the church at Corinth, "For we do not want you to be ignorant, brethren, of our trouble which came to us in Asia: that we were burdened beyond measure, above strength, so that we despaired even of life" (1 Cor. 1:8).

Even John the Baptist had his moments of doubt. After he was arrested, unsure of whether Jesus was indeed the Messiah, he sent word to

Jesus from prison, "Are You the Coming One, or do we look for another?" (Matt. 11:3).

And dare I say it? Even Jesus struggled. He never doubted the Father. But did He struggle with the Father's plan? Absolutely. We've already seen how, in the Garden of Gethsemane, His sweat became like drops of blood, and He prayed, "Father, if it is Your will, take this cup away from Me; nevertheless not My will, but Yours, be done" (Luke 22:42). Yet even as He was temporarily forsaken, He called on His Father: " 'My God, My God why have you forsaken Me?' " (Mark 15:34).

In contrast, we as Christians never will be forsaken, but we may feel like we have been sometimes. Therefore, it is in these times that we need to call on the Lord. And when we don't understand what God is doing, we fall back on what we do understand: that He loves us, He is looking out for our best interests, and He is making us more like Jesus.

IT'S NOT OVER YET

So, you're not the only one who deals with doubt and skepticism sometimes. But remember, it's not over 'til it's over. Just ask Joseph, who was sold by his brothers into slavery in Egypt, wrongly accused, and thrown into prison, only to rise to a position of great power and influence in Egypt that enabled him to save his entire family. Just ask Daniel, Shadrach, Meshech, and Abed-Nego, whose bold stand for their faith landed them in a lion's den and a fiery furnace, respectively. Yet God miraculously intervened and spared their lives. Just ask Peter, who was arrested and thrown into prison, only to be freed by an angel during the night. Just ask Martha, who buried her brother Lazarus, only to see Jesus resurrect him. And just ask the disciples, who saw their Lord arrested, tried, and crucified....

There are times when we must completely ignore our emotions and simply take God at His Word.

Jesus had been taken away unexpectedly, and this had come as a complete shock to them. Many of His disciples thought He was about to set up His kingdom then and there. But instead, He was nailed to a cross. Now there were scattered reports that He was alive! Mary Magdalene had met the risen Lord near the tomb and had told the others.

Jesus then appeared to two discouraged disciples
on the road to Emmaus. They came back and told
the disciples how Jesus had met them and talked
with them. And then … guess who came to dinner?

> Then, the same day at evening, being the
> first day of the week, when the doors were
> shut where the disciples were assembled,
> for fear of the Jews, Jesus came and stood in
> the midst, and said to them, "Peace be with
> you." When He had said this, He showed
> them His hands and His side. Then the
> disciples were glad when they saw the Lord.
> So Jesus said to them again, "Peace to you!
> As the Father has sent Me, I also send you."
> And when He had said this, He breathed on
> them, and said to them, "Receive the Holy
> Spirit." (vv. 20–22)

Now that Christ had died and risen, His work
was complete. The Holy Spirit was now coming
into the disciples, which Jesus had promised
earlier: "And I will pray the Father, and He will
give you another Helper, that He may abide with
you forever—the Spirit of truth, whom the world
cannot receive, because it neither sees Him nor
knows Him; but you know Him, for He dwells
with you and will be in you" (John 14:16–17).
The same is true when we put our faith in Christ.

Ephesians 1:13–14 tells us, "In Him you also trusted, after you heard the word of truth, the gospel of your salvation; in whom you were sealed with the Holy Spirit of promise, who is the guarantee of our inheritance...."

Thomas didn't ask for anything more than what the others had seen.

There also was another dimension of power that was to come upon the disciples on Pentecost: " 'But you shall receive power when the Holy Spirit has come upon you; and you shall be witnesses to Me in Jerusalem, and in all Judea and Samaria, and to the end of the earth' " (Acts 1:8). Jesus made an interesting statement to them here as well: "If you forgive the sins of any, they are forgiven them; if you retain the sins of any, they are retained" (v. 23). Clearly, God hasn't given us the ability to forgive the sins of others. As Jesus said, "Who can forgive sins but God alone?" (Mark 2:7). Having said that, we are His representatives. As we proclaim the gospel and people believe, we have the authority, as His representatives, to tell them, "Your sin is forgiven." Often after praying with people to accept Christ, I will do this. I'll tell them, "If you meant that prayer you just prayed, then on the authority of God's Word, your sins are forgiven."

Jesus was saying, "If you *forgive the sins* of any, they are forgiven them" (v. 23, emphasis mine). I remember meeting a man who was struggling with a great deal of guilt in his life. I spent a lot of time talking and praying with him and reminding him of what the Bible said: "If we confess our sins, He is faithful and just to forgive us our sins and to cleanse us from all unrighteousness" (1 John 1:9). We must recognize there are times when we must completely ignore our emotions and simply take God at His Word, because "if our heart condemns us, God is greater than our heart, and knows all things" (1 John 3:20).

At the same time, if people haven't met God's requirements, we must tell them their sin is *not* forgiven: "If you retain the sins of any, they are retained" (v. 23). For example, someone may say, "I don't want Christ. I will do whatever I want." And our response should be, "Unless you repent, you will face the repercussions."

The risen Lord personally appeared to the disciples, the Holy Spirit was breathed on them, and a charge was given to represent Him. It was quite a meeting—a bad day to miss church. But one of them did: Thomas.

WHY WE NEED EACH OTHER

Like the others, Thomas was devastated by the crucifixion of Jesus. And in his personal pain, he withdrew not only from God, but from others. But when we are hurting, that is the time we should be seeking out the fellowship of God's people. So when the disciples saw Thomas, they probably said, "You should have been there last night!"

Faith never means gullibility.

What a mistake we make when we neglect fellowship with God's people. That, too, was the problem with the two discouraged disciples on the Emmaus Road. They wanted to put as much distance as possible between themselves and the cross. But after Jesus appeared, the first thing they did was return to the believers. And Thomas had missed out on an appearance of the Lord himself.

> Now Thomas, called the Twin, one of the
> twelve, was not with them when Jesus came.
> The other disciples therefore said to him,
> "We have seen the Lord." So he said to
> them, "Unless I see in His hands the print
> of the nails, and put my finger into the print
> of the nails, and put my hand into His side, I
> will not believe." (vv. 24–25)

AN HONEST REQUEST

No one could ever accuse Thomas of failing to
think for himself. He certainly was an individual,
not willing to simply believe what others said or
experienced. Thomas wanted to know for himself.
And there is nothing wrong with that. How easily
Jesus could have ignored Thomas altogether, seeing
that he wasn't even present with the disciples when
He appeared: "Hey, Buddy, you snooze, you lose!
Show up next time!" But Jesus condescended to
Thomas' personal doubts and skepticism, and He
lovingly offered him personal proof:

> And after eight days His disciples were
> again inside, and Thomas with them. Jesus
> came, the doors being shut, and stood in the
> midst, and said, "Peace to you!" Then He
> said to Thomas, "Reach your finger here,
> and look at My hands; and reach your hand

here, and put it into My side. Do not be
unbelieving, but believing." And Thomas
answered and said to Him, "My Lord and
my God!" (John 20:26–28)

Jesus does that with countless others, coming
to where they are, lovingly offering personal proof
of His love for them. And He will meet you where
you are right now. When I first came to Christ, I
was filled with doubt and skepticism. I said to God,
"If You are real, then You need to make yourself
real to me!" It wasn't rebellion on my part or even
a challenge to God, per se. It was a plea, a cry for
God to help a hardened, skeptical, cynical young
man. And He did.

Thomas didn't ask for anything more than what
the others had seen. He didn't ask for a special
revelation. He simply asked for the same proof.
Eight days had passed. He had missed out, and he
wanted personal proof. And though we can argue
the fact that he wanted to personally see the risen
Lord, everyone needs to internalize their own
faith—not live off the faith of others.

Sometimes Christian parents are alarmed
when their children get a little older and perhaps
challenge what they have always taught them:
"Mom, how do you know Jesus is the only way

to God?"; "Dad, how can we be sure the Bible
is the Word of God?"; "What about evolution?"
Questions like these can make parents feel as
though they somehow failed. But as I've pointed
out, "Doubt is not always a sign that a man is
wrong. It may be a sign that he is thinking." So in
times like these, parents need to dig into God's
Word and help their children understand these
truths. They need to believe them, not just because
their parents do, but because they have integrated
them into their own lives.

*You cannot effectively
walk with Christ solo.*

All Thomas wanted was to know for himself.
Thomas was no wallflower, after all. He was
courageous and bold. After Lazarus died, Jesus
told the disciples they needed to go and wake him
up. The disciples were confused and thought Jesus
meant that Lazarus was sleeping when, in fact, he
was dead. When Jesus told them they were going to
Lazarus, Thomas said, "Let us go that we may die
with Him" (John 11:16). Jesus wasn't requiring any
such thing; yet Thomas was willing to lay his life

down. Let's not forget that Thomas was martyred for his faith. According to church history, he was preaching in India and was told to stop, but when he refused, he was speared to death. So Thomas was an authentic follower of Jesus. We might criticize him, but he didn't deny Jesus as Simon Peter had. He just wanted to know for himself, and once he knew, he was committed. Not only was Thomas bold and courageous, but he also thought for himself.

A LITTLE SKEPTICISM CAN BE GOOD

There is nothing wrong with a little healthy skepticism today. Far too often, Christians can be the most gullible people of all. We want to believe the best of everyone, and that is indeed biblical. Yet the Bible also warns there will be false teachers and false miracles. Therefore, we are to "test all things; hold fast what is good" (1 Thess. 5:21). We are also told, "Do not believe every spirit, but test the spirits, whether they are of God; because many false prophets have gone out into this world" (1 John 4:1). As A.W. Tozer observed, "In our constant struggle to believe, we are likely to overlook the simple fact that a bit of healthy disbelief is sometimes as needful as faith to the welfare of our souls. … " It is not a sin to doubt some things, but it may be fatal to believe everything. Faith never means gullibility. Some Christians can be simply foolish, feeling that because they must believe certain things, they must believe everything.

Thomas was not that kind of believer. We already know the famous question Thomas asked when Jesus told the disciples, "In My Father's house are many mansions; if it were not so, I would have told you. I go to prepare a place for you. … And where I go you know, and the way you know" (John 14:2, 4).

Grace is giving us what we don't deserve.

It is also worth noting that Jesus did not appear to Thomas until he was present with other believers. Some people say, "Who needs church? The Man Upstairs and I are friends; we don't need to meet in some dark, old church building. I can talk to God while I'm out surfing or golfing." But know this: Jesus is present in a special way when believers gather together." Jesus said, "For where two or three are gathered together in My name, I am there in the midst of them" (Matt. 18:20). This is why you cannot effectively walk with Christ solo. I tried to do that as a young believer and discovered it was a no man's land.

THE GIFT OF GRACE

So the disciples were gathered together, Thomas was with them, and Jesus appears, greeting them with the familiar Jewish phrase, "*Shalom*," or "Peace to you!" How easily He could have greeted them with rebuke! How they deserved it! He could have reminded them of their unfaithfulness and fear the previous weekend. He could have laid them all off and hired a new set of disciples. But grace is giving us what we don't deserve. The Bible says, "He has not dealt with us according to our sins, nor punished us according to our iniquities" (Ps. 103:11). Jesus lovingly said, "Peace to you!"

Jesus had been listening in on the earlier conversation between Thomas and the others. It reminds me of a plaque I once saw, which read:

> Christ is the head of this household,The unseen guest at every meal,The unseen listener to every conversation.

So Jesus essentially was saying, "OK, Thomas. I heard what you said. Reach your finger here, and look at My hands! Reach your hand here into My side!" It seems Jesus made this appearance especially for Thomas, which reminds us that God cares about us as individuals. David wrote, "O Lord, you have examined my heart and know everything about me ... " (Ps. 139:1 NLT).

Skepticism is open to believing, but unbelief is refusing to believe.

Upon seeing the risen and living Lord, Thomas' skepticism gave way to belief: "My Lord and my God!" This is the difference between skepticism and unbelief. Skepticism is open to believing, but unbelief is refusing to believe. Skepticism is honesty; unbelief is stubbornness. Skepticism is looking for light, while unbelief is content with darkness. Unbelievers have no intention of changing or believing. They will offer up a well-worn excuse, but the fact of the matter is that even when confronted with evidence to refute their unbelief, they reject it out of hand. That is because they do not want to believe.

GOD IN THEIR MIDST

Up to this point, no doubt, Thomas admired Jesus as a tremendous hero, role model, and messenger of God, but now He was his Lord and his God. It is not enough to acknowledge Him as God, but *your* God. The Bible tells us that "Even the demons believe—and tremble!" (James 2:19).

Also notice that Jesus accepted this worship from Thomas. When God led Peter to bring the gospel to the searching Cornelius, he fell at Peter's feet. But Peter corrected him: "Stand up; I myself am also a man" (Acts 10:26). Peter would not accept worship or allow someone to bow before him. That was for God alone.

When Paul and Barnabas performed a miracle by the hand of God in Lystra, the people began ripping off their clothes and worshipping them. But Paul said, "Friends, why are you doing this? We are merely human beings like yourselves!" (Acts 14:15 NLT).

Jesus, however, accepted the worship of Thomas, who addressed Him as "My Lord and my God!" When He was being tempted in the wilderness, Jesus rebuked the devil and said, " 'You shall worship the Lord your God, and

Him only you shall serve' " (Luke 4:8). Jesus was God, and therefore rightfully accepted Thomas' worship. So much for those who argue that Jesus never claimed to be God.

JESUS' BLESSING FOR US

Jesus then offered a word of encouragement and a special blessing for us today: "Jesus said to him, 'Thomas, because you have seen Me, you have believed. Blessed are those who have not seen and yet have believed' " (John 20:29). It is important for us to know that God loves to bless us. Jesus both began and concluded His earthly ministry with blessing people. When children came to Him, He took them in His arms and blessed them. And Luke's Gospel tells us that after His resurrection, "He led them [the disciples] out as far as Bethany, and He lifted up His hands and blessed them" (Luke 24:50).

But does this mean that a faith that has not seen, and yet has believed, is the only kind of faith that is blessed? Of course not. John himself tells us, "And truly Jesus did many other signs in the presence of His disciples, which are not written in this book; but these are written that you may believe that Jesus is the Christ, the Son of God, and that believing you may have life in His name" (vv. 30–31).

So obviously, Jesus isn't speaking of a subjective faith, but a satisfied faith. He is speaking of a faith that is satisfied with what God gives rather than one that focuses on what He doesn't. The Bible is filled with accounts of visions, signs, wonders, and spiritual gifts at work. Perhaps we have longed for a vision of an angel or a miracle in our own lives. That isn't a bad thing, necessarily.

Seeing and experiencing miracles does not guarantee a strong faith.

When I first became a Christian, that is what I wanted: a miracle-filled life. I wanted a personal word from the Lord (audibly if possible) every day, like an operative on *Mission Impossible*: "Good morning, Greg. Your mission, should you choose to accept it, is. ... " I wanted signs and wonders and emotional experiences. After a time, I discovered the Christian life is a life of faith, not feeling. The Bible says, "The just shall live by faith" (Rom. 1:17).

Some Christians want these things to the extent that they become a distraction. Consider this:

believers should not follow after signs and wonders; signs and wonders should follow after them.

Seeing and experiencing miracles does not guarantee a strong faith. Pharaoh saw many miracles, but his heart only became harder. The children of Israel saw dramatic ones as well, but they rebelled. The church of Corinth was awash in miracles—and also in rampant immorality. I am not attempting to denigrate miracles, signs, and wonders. God can bring them where and when He desires, and when He does, we are to thank Him. But we also are to be thankful for what we presently have—and apply it in our lives. As A. B. Simpson wrote,

> Once it was the blessing, Now it is the Lord;
> Once it was the feeling, Now it is His Word.
> Once His gifts I wanted, Now the Giver own;
> Once I sought for healing, Now Himself alone. [1]

Now, we have not seen Jesus … yet. But "blessed are those who have not seen and yet have believed" (v. 29). There is coming a day when every eye shall see Him. There is coming a day when every knee shall bow. Until then, we are to believe.

Mark's Gospel tells the story of a distraught father who brought his demon-possessed child to Jesus. "If You can do anything, have compassion on us and help us," he told Jesus.

Jesus answered, "If you can believe, all things are possible to him who believes."

So the man prayed an honest prayer: "Lord, I believe; help my unbelief!" (Mark 9:24).

You might be a skeptic today, like I once was. You may say, like Thomas, "Show me, and I'll believe." But Jesus essentially says, "Believe, and I'll show you," and "Call to Me, and I will answer you and show you great and mighty things, which you do not know" (Jer. 33:3). Just come to God with your doubts, questions, and even your skepticism, and say, "Lord, come into my life. Forgive me of my sins."

I am not promising that if you become a Christian, you will have a perfect life. I am not saying that if you follow Jesus, you never will go through a hardship. But I am saying this: you never will be alone. You will find peace and purpose and meaning in your life, and you will go to heaven when you die. If that is not a happy ending, then I don't know what is. And it is yours today...if you will believe.

11 | BREAKFAST WITH JESUS

John 21:1–17

Have you ever failed miserably in life? Maybe it was in your education, in your business, in a relationship, or even a marriage. Maybe you've experienced one failure after another. Or perhaps you have failed in your spiritual life. You had high hopes of what you were going to do and how you were going to live as a follower of Jesus Christ. But you failed. As a result, you've even begun to wonder whether you really are a child of God. You wonder if you truly love the Lord.

Who actually plans on walking away from God?

If so, then you're in good company, because no one less than the apostle Peter felt this way after he denied the Lord. Yet before us is a story of God's forgiveness. And not only that, it is a story of God's recommissioning when Simon Peter had breakfast with Jesus. Here we'll also discover five litmus tests for determining what it really is to love the Lord. And we'll look at a question Jesus asked on this particular morning that, in a sense, He is still asking some two thousand years later.

THE BACKWARD SLIDE

At this point in time, we know that Peter had clearly backslidden. Of course, that hadn't been his plan, but that is what happened. Who actually *plans* on walking away from God? It is not something that generally happens overnight. Instead, it's a number of steps over a period of time that ultimately lead up to it. For Peter, it all fell apart in the Upper Room when Jesus spoke of the one who would betray Him, and also said the disciples would forsake Him. Shocked to hear Jesus say that all of them would forsake Him, Peter just had to separate himself from the rabble and protest: "Even if all fall away, I will not.... Even if I have to die with you, I will never disown you" (Mark 14:29, 31 NIV). In other words, "Lord, with all due respect, that simply is not going to happen! You can depend on me, no matter what! I will be there for You always!"But Jesus knew Peter better than Peter knew himself. Peter fell asleep in Gethsemane instead of praying as Jesus had asked him to, oblivious to the obvious anguish that Jesus was experiencing. And though he wasn't so good in the prayer department, when the soldiers came to arrest Jesus, he found something he could handle. He drew his sword, ready to defend his Lord. But even in this, Peter failed.

There is futility and uselessness in living our lives without the direction and blessing of Jesus.

Then, as they led Jesus away, he followed at a distance, his short-lived courage quickly giving way to raw fear. Then came that terrible moment when he did just what Jesus said he would do: he denied the Lord. His eyes met the eyes of Jesus for a moment—a moment that seemed like an eternity. And then Jesus was whisked away and tried. The last sight he had of his Lord was hanging on a cross, so beaten and bloodied that He was scarcely recognizable.

So Peter's whole world had come crumbling down around him.

BEGINNING AGAIN

But the Resurrection changed all of that. Imagine Peter's shock and surprise when he heard that Jesus not only had risen from the dead, but had sent a message, "But go, tell his disciples and Peter, 'He is going ahead of you into Galilee. There you will see him, just as he told you'" (Mark 16:7 NIV). So John and Peter ran to the tomb and found it empty. Peter didn't know what to think. And now Jesus would recommission Peter and reassure him of His love and plan for his life.

*Sometimes success
can be a form of failure.*

As our story begins, it was *déjá vu* time for the disciples. They had fished all night and caught nothing. But in their defense, they didn't know what to do at this point. The Lord had risen, and they were uncertain about their future. So they went fishing. How many times have you wanted to get away from your problems and heartaches and just hang out the sign, "Gone fishing"? Jesus would use this failure to once again prove a vital point: there is futility and uselessness in living our lives without the direction and blessing of Jesus. We foolishly try to keep God out of our lives, and we blindly pursue our plans and passions. Many times God will not let you have everything you want. But then there are times when He will. As George Bernard Shaw said, "There are two sources of unhappiness in life. One is not getting what you want. The other is getting it." We can end up like Solomon, who said,

> "Anything I wanted, I took. I did not restrain myself from any joy. I even found great pleasure in hard work, an additional reward for all my labors. But as I looked at everything I had worked so hard to accomplish, it was all so meaningless. It was like chasing the wind. There was nothing really worthwhile anywhere."
> (Eccl. 2:10–11 NLT)

Sometimes success can be a form of failure, meaning, what cost was paid to achieve that success? Did it require using deception and betrayal? Did it mean abandoning your principles and sacrificing your integrity? Did it involve neglecting your family and friends? Did it entail forgetting about—or in some cases, outright abandoning—God? When the children of Israel tested God in the desert, the Bible says, "And He gave them their request, but sent leanness into their soul" (Ps. 106:15). We can do worse than fail. We can succeed and be too proud of our success. We can succeed and worship the accomplishment rather than the One who helped us reach it. We can succeed and forget whose Hand it is to give or to withhold. Success—even spiritual success— can be destructive, while failure can become an unspeakable benefit.

Failure can become
an unspeakable benefit.

Jesus wanted to help His disciples, but first they would need to learn a valuable lesson. So He called to them from the shore: "Children [boys], have you any food?" (v. 5). First, He asked a question, the basis for which was the need to show the disciples their own need and failure. God did the same thing in the Garden of Eden after

Adam had eaten the forbidden fruit: "Have you eaten from the tree of which I commanded you that you should not eat?" (Gen. 3:11). God wanted acknowledgement and confession from Adam, not excuses. To Elijah, who had run away in terror after receiving a death threat from Queen Jezebel, God posed the question, "What are you doing here, Elijah?" (1 Kings 19:9). And now to His disciples, Jesus was saying, "Well, boys, are the fish biting?" In other words, had they been successful? Were they satisfied? Were they willing to admit their failure? Before we can find God's forgiveness and His restoration, we must first admit our need. That means no excuses, and no blaming others—just honest confession as we take responsibility for our own actions.

So Jesus offered a solution. He said, "Cast the net on the right side of the boat, and you will find some" (v. 6). This would remind Simon Peter of an earlier encounter with Jesus at the Lake of Gennesaret, when Jesus told him, "Launch out into the deep, and let down your nets for a catch" (Luke 5:4). And just as it happened then, it happened again. The net was filled to capacity with fish. John, the spiritually perceptive one, recognized what was happening. "It is the Lord!" he told Peter. So Peter impulsively flung himself into the water and swam toward the shore. By this time, the disciples would have been about 300 feet out. John tells us,

> The other disciples followed in the boat, towing the net full of fish, for they were not far from shore, about a hundred yards. When they landed, they saw a fire of burning coals there with fish on it, and some bread. Jesus said to them, "Bring some of the fish you have just caught." Simon Peter climbed aboard and dragged the net ashore. … Jesus said to them, "Come and have breakfast." (vv. 9–12 NIV)

Before we can find God's forgiveness and His restoration, we must first admit our need.

Was this not an inviting scene? Jesus was thoughtful, even in the smallest matters. Imagine, the Creator of the universe in human form, who had just been crucified and was now resurrected, was serving breakfast to His disciples! Instead of simply creating fish, He went through the effort of using the fish that were caught. God doesn't need our participation, but He wants it. He didn't need the boy's lunch of five loaves and two fishes to feed a hungry multitude, but He used it anyway. And He wants to use what we have so we can participate in His working.

ONE QUESTION, THREE WAYS

Now, we come to the first of three profound questions Jesus had for Peter: "Simon, son of Jonah, do you love Me more than these?" (v. 15). Interesting. The way we determine someone's spirituality is by his or her doctrine, or faith, or even personal obedience to the Word of God. And these are all very valid things, but they are not necessarily the most important. Jesus didn't ask, "Are you doctrinally correct?" or "Do you have faith?" or "Have you been obedient?" Rather, He asked, "Do you love me?" Why is this question so important? Because if you really love the Lord, you will want to be doctrinally correct, studying His Word. If you really love the Lord, you will *want to* grow in faith. If you really love the Lord, you will *want to* obey Him. And if these things don't follow your love for God, then it isn't real love. It would be like saying, "I love my wife," but then not wanting to spend time with her. It would be like saying, "I'm in love with my husband," but then being repeatedly unfaithful to him. That isn't love. So Jesus wanted to put first things first: "Do you love Me?"

His love is ever-consistent and unchanging, regardless of the circumstances.

Peter arrived on shore, dripping wet, yet filled with excitement to see the risen Lord. At the same time, he was feeling a deep shame for his sins. As they sat around the fire, there was an awkward silence. Peter's thoughts probably flashed back to the glow of another fire. There, he had denied the Lord. Jesus broke the silence and asked, "Simon son of Jonah, do you love Me more than these?" It's interesting to note Jesus' choice of words: "Simon, son of Jonah," as compared to his new name, Simon Peter. Jesus would use his names interchangeably, depending on how he was behaving.

So Jesus proceeded to test Peter three times to see if he had really learned anything from his failure. Peter had denied the Lord three times, and now he would be tested three times. In the original language, the word "love" Jesus used came from the Greek word *agape*. It is an all-consuming, dedicated, sacrificial love. We get our English word "agony" from it. So Jesus was saying, "Peter, do you *agape* Me? Do you have this all-consuming, sacrificial total love?" Or a simpler way of stating it, "Peter, do you love Me 100 percent?"

"Lord, I *phileo* you," Peter responds. In other words, "Lord, I love you with a 60 percent love."

Peter wasn't saying that he didn't love Jesus. He simply wasn't boasting of His love for the Lord any longer. And that is a good thing for us to remember. Our love can be fickle and moody at times. But His love is ever-consistent and unchanging, regardless of the circumstances. God said, "Yes, I have loved you with an everlasting love; therefore with lovingkindness I have drawn you (Jer. 31:3). John wrote, "How great is the love the Father has lavished on us, that we should be called children of God!" (1 John 3:1 NIV), and "We love Him because He first loved us" (1 John 4:19 NIV). When we sin, like Peter, we are tempted to believe that we have no love for Christ. But let this story encourage you.

It's impossible for any true lovers of God to pursue an endless course of sin, but it is quite possible for them to stumble in sin, although they will be miserable there.

In essence, Jesus was asking Peter, "Do you love Me?" And Peter was saying that He loved Him like a friend. Remember, guys, back in high school when you would say to a girl, "I'm in love with you. Do you love me?"

She would sweetly reply, "I *like* you a lot. I love you like a friend!" Translation: "Forget about it."

I think Jesus is still asking this probing question today: "Do you love Me?" So what does it really mean when we say we love the Lord? Is it simply an over-sentimental emotion we experience, or is it more? Love is more than an emotion. It's a commitment.

Jesus accepted Peter's answer and commissioned him to service: "Feed My lambs" (v. 15). He was saying, "Peter, up to this point, you have been a fisher of men. Now you are going to be a keeper of lambs. I'm calling you not only to speak to this world, but to take care of My sheep." No greater honor could have been bestowed upon Simon Peter.

Then came a second question from the Lord: "Simon, son of Jonah, do you love Me?" (v. 16).

"Yes, Lord; You know that I love You," Peter told Him.

The second question was a variation on the first: "Do you love me *more than these*?" (v. 15, emphasis mine). Jesus was essentially saying, "Simon, are you still boastful and proud?" Peter was not. He had learned his lesson well. So now Jesus was simply asking, "Okay, Simon. Do you love Me?"

Again, Peter would not commit to the word *agape*, and instead said he loved Jesus like a close friend. Fair enough. Jesus accepted his answer and again affirmed him by saying, "Tend My sheep."

Love is more than an emotion. It's a commitment.

So now we come to the third and final test: " 'Simon, son of Jonah, do you love Me?' Peter was grieved because He said to him the third time, 'Do you love Me?' " (v. 17). This time, the word Jesus used for "love" was the same word Peter had used: *phileo*. He was essentially saying, "Simon, are you sure you love Me like a friend? Have you thought this through? Are you positive about it?"

This irritated Peter, and he said, "Lord, You know all things; You know that I love You." In Peter's previous affirmation of Jesus' omniscience in verses 15–16, he used a strong Greek word that meant Jesus knew every detail. But in his third and final answer, he changed words, using a term that conveyed intimate, personal knowledge, as if to say, "Lord, You know me better than I know myself! You have walked with me. You know me personally in every way. You know all things! To the best of my understanding, I really do love You as a friend!" God knows the same about us as well.

So Jesus again affirmed Simon Peter by saying, "Feed My sheep" (v. 17). In other words, "Good answer, Simon. Good answer."

SIGNS THAT A PERSON LOVES GOD

In a sense, Jesus is still asking this question today: Do you love Me? Most of us would quickly answer that we love God, but let's take a test from Scripture. What are some of the earmarks of a person who truly loves God and is growing in that love for Him?

A person who loves the Lord will long for personal communion with Him. David wrote,

> My soul thirsts for you, my body longs for you, in a dry and weary land where there is no water. I have seen you in the sanctuary and beheld your power and your glory. Because your love is better than life, my lips will glorify you. I will praise you as long as I live, and in your name I will lift up my hands. My soul will be satisfied as with the richest of foods; with singing lips my mouth will praise you. On my bed I remember you; I think of you through the watches of the night. (Ps. 63:1–6 NIV)

Jesus is still asking this question today: Do you love Me?

When your heart overflows with love for God, you will delight in worship and praise. When you're really in love with someone, you will delight to be in his or her presence. When you hear of husbands and wives who are spending less and less time together, spending more time with their friends, and taking separate vacations, this is a warning signal.

A person who loves the Lord will in turn love the things that He loves. We know what God loves by what He has declared to us in His Word. The psalmist declared, "Oh, how I love your law! I meditate on it all day long" (Ps. 119:97 NIV). Do you love the Word of God? Do you love His church? Do you love lost people? God does.

A person who loves the Lord will in turn hate the things that He hates. As we grow in our love for the Lord, His nature will become our nature. Psalm 97:10 says, "You who love the Lord, hate evil! He preserves the souls of His saints; He delivers them out of the hand of the wicked." God hates sin, and so should we. The Bible tells us, "Abhor what is evil. Cling to what is good" (Rom. 12:9). The problem is, we are often fascinated by evil. We are drawn to it, first as an observer, and then as a participator. But instead of flirting with evil, we need to run from it.

A person who loves the Lord will long for Christ's return. The apostle Paul rejoiced in what the future had in store: "And now the prize awaits me—the crown of righteousness that the Lord, the righteous Judge, will give me on that great day of his return. And the prize is not just for me but for

all who eagerly look forward to his glorious return"
(2 Timothy 4:8 NLT).

Instead of flirting with evil,
we need to run from it.

Finally, a person who loves the Lord will keep
His commandments. Jesus said, "Whoever has my
commands and obeys them, he is the one who loves
me. He who loves me will be loved by my Father,
and I too will love him and show myself to him"
(John 14:21 NIV). And He also asked, "Why do you
call Me 'Lord, Lord,' and not do the things which
I say?" (Luke 6:46).

So not only was Peter forgiven of his sins, but he
was recommissioned for service. Perhaps you have
failed recently. Maybe you have done things you are
ashamed of. You know what Peter must have felt like
that morning at the Sea of Tiberias, reluctant to look
at Jesus. Perhaps you even have been reluctant to
go to church—or to pick up this book. But Jesus is
asking you today, "Do you love Me?" If you do, then
get on with the business of walking with and obeying
Him. These things cannot take the place of love, but
if you truly love Him, then you should do them.

God can and will forgive and restore you as well if you come to Him now. But you must acknowledge your true condition, which is that you are a sinner who is separated from God. Then you need to be sorry for your sin and turn from it. As 1 John 1:19 promises, "If we confess our sins, He is faithful and just to forgive us our sins and to cleanse us from all unrighteousness."

Just as Jesus called from the shore to the disciples, "Come and dine!", He is calling you right now. On other occasions, Jesus used a similar phrase. When two of John the Baptist's disciples began to follow Him out of curiosity and then asked where He lived, Jesus responded, "Come and see!" (John 1:39).

Perhaps you're curious right now. You want to know more about Jesus Christ. If so, He says, "Come and see for yourself!"

Maybe you're tired right now. Jesus said, "Come to Me, all you who labor and are heavy laden, and I will give you rest" (Matt. 11:28). He says, "Come and rest."

Then again, perhaps your life hasn't been what you had hoped it would. Have you been pulling up a lot of empty nets? Then it's time to let Jesus come on board.

Come and see.
Come and dine.
Come and rest.
Come now.

AFTERWORD

The First Steps toward Living Out Your Faith

If you want to begin the journey of living out your faith, but don't know where to start, if you don't have the assurance that you will go to heaven when you die, if you are still carrying a load of guilt around, but want to be forgiven, then here is what you need to do:

1. *Realize that you are a sinner.* No matter how good of a life we try to live, we still fall miserably short of being a good person. That is because we are all sinners. We all fall short of God's desire for us to be holy. The Bible says, "No one is good—not even one" (Romans 3:10 NLT). This is because we cannot become who we are supposed to be without Jesus Christ.

2. *Recognize that Jesus Christ died on the cross for you.* The Bible tells us, "But God showed His great love for us by sending Christ to die for us while were still sinners" (Rom 5:8 NLT). This is the Good News, that God loves us so much that, when we least deserved it, He sent His only Son to die in our place.

3. *Repent of your sin.* The Bible tells us to "repent and be converted" (Acts 3:19). The word, "repent," means "to change our direction in life." Instead of running away from God, we can run toward Him.

4. *Receive Jesus Christ into your life.* Becoming a Christian is not merely believing some creed or going to church on Sunday. It is having Christ himself take residence in your life and heart. Jesus said, "Behold, I stand at the door [of your life] and knock. If anyone hears My voice and opens the door, I will come in . . ." (Rev. 3:20).

If you would like to invite Christ into your life, simply pray a prayer like this one, and mean it in your heart:

Dear Lord Jesus, I know I am a sinner. I believe you died for my sins. Right now, I turn from my sins and open the door of my heart and life. I confess you as my personal Lord and Savior. Thank you for saving me. Amen.

The Bible tells us, "If we confess our sins, He is faithful and just to forgive us our sins and cleanse us from all unrighteousness" (1 John 1:9). If you just prayed that prayer and meant it, then Jesus Christ has now taken residence in your heart.

Your decision to follow Christ means God has forgiven you and that you will spend eternity in heaven. It means you will be ready to meet Christ when He returns.

To help you grow in your newfound faith, be sure to make the following a part of your life each day: read the Bible regularly, pray, spend time with other Christians by going to church, and tell others about your faith in Christ.

For additional resources to help you learn more about what it means to be a follower of Jesus Christ and to live out your faith, please visit http://www. harvest.org/knowgod/.

NOTES

CHAPTER 2
"GOD'S CURE FOR HEART TROUBLE"

1. Kathleen Fackelmann, "Stress Can Ravage the Body, Unless the Mind Says No," USA TODAY, March 31, 2005, http://www.usatoday.com/news/health/2005-03-21-stress_x.htm.

2. "Mommy Madness: Motherhood in the Age of Anxiety," *Single Mom.com*, http://www.singlemom.com/DAYTODAY/balancing/book_mommy_madness.htm.

3. Karen Pallarito, "Stressed Out and Sick About It," *ABC News*, February 12, 2005, http://abcnews.go.com/Health/Healthology/story?id=493978.

4. "Poll: Americans Worry about Nuclear Weapons," *MSNBC.com*, March 30, 2005, http://www.msnbc.msn.com/id/7340591/from/RL.1/.

5. Ibid.

6. C. S. Lewis, *The Problem of Pain* (San Francisco: HarperCollins, 2001), 151.

CHAPTER 5
"JESUS' PRAYER FOR YOU"

1. Skip Heitzig, *When God Prays* (Wheaton, Ill.: Tyndale House Publishers, 2003, 58–59.

2. Ibid, p. 37.

CHAPTER 6
"THE PURPOSE IN GETHSEMANE"

1. Alfred Edersheim, *The Life and Times of Jesus the Messiah*. Book V: The Cross and the Crown. Philologos Religious Online Books. http://www.kjvuser.com/lifeandtimes/book512.htm.

2. Ella Wilcox, "Quotes by Ella Wilcox," *Zaadz.com*, http://www.zaadz.com/quotes/authors/ella_wilcox (accessed March 6, 2006).

CHAPTER 9
"A NEW BEGINNING"

1. Rhea F. Miller, "I'd Rather Have Jesus," 1939.

CHAPTER 10
"JESUS AND THE SKEPTIC"

1. A. B. Simpson, "Himself," *Biblebelievers. com*, http://www.biblebelievers.com/simpson-ab_himself.html (accessed March 13, 2006).

ABOUT THE AUTHOR

Greg Laurie is the pastor of Harvest Christian Fellowship (one of America's largest churches) in Riverside, California. He is the author of over thirty books, including the Gold Medallion Award winner, *The Upside-Down Church*, as well as *Every Day with Jesus; Marriage Connections; Losers and Winners, Saints and Sinners; Dealing with Giants;* and *Are These the Last Days?* You can find his study notes in the *New Believer's Bible* and the *Seeker's Bible*. Host of the *Harvest: Greg Laurie* television program and the nationally syndicated radio program, *A New Beginning*, Greg Laurie is also the founder and featured speaker for Harvest Crusades—contemporary, large-scale evangelistic outreaches, which local churches organize nationally and internationally. He and his wife Cathe have two children and live in Southern California.

Other AllenDavid books
published by Kerygma Publishing

The Great Compromise

For Every Season: Daily Devotions

Strengthening Your Marriage

Marriage Connections

Are We Living in the Last Days?

"I'm Going on a Diet Tomorrow"

Strengthening Your Faith

Deepening Your Faith

Dealing with Giants

Secrets to Spiritual Success

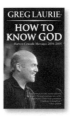

How to Know God

Visit: www.kerygmapublishing.com
www.allendavidbooks.com
www.harvest.org